On the *Revival of the Religious Sciences* (*Iḥyāʾ ʿulūm al-dīn*)

"The *Iḥyāʾ ʿulūm al-dīn* is the most valuable and most beautiful of books."

—Ibn Khallikān (d. 681/1282)

"The *Iḥyāʾ ʿulūm al-dīn* is one of al-Ghazālī's best works."

—Aḥmad b. ʿAbd al-Ḥalīm (d. 728/1328)

"Any seeker of [felicity of] the hereafter cannot do without the *Iḥyāʾ ʿulūm al-dīn*"

—Tāj al-Dīn al-Subkī (d. 771/1370)

"The *Iḥyāʾ ʿulūm al-dīn* is a marvelous book containing a wide variety of Islamic sciences intermixed with many subtle accounts of Sufism and matters of the heart."

—Ibn Kathīr (d. 774/1373)

"The *Iḥyāʾ ʿulūm al-dīn* is one of best and greatest books on admonition, it was said concerning it, 'if all the books of Islam were lost except for the *Iḥyāʾ* it would suffice what was lost.'"

—Ḥājjī Khalīfa Kātib Čelebī (d. 1067/1657)

"The *Iḥyāʾ* [*ʿulūm al-dīn*] is one of [Imām al-Ghazālī's] most noble works, his most famous work, and by far his greatest work'"

—Muḥammad Murtaḍā l-Zabīdī (d. 1205/1791)

On Imām al-Ghazālī

"Al-Ghazālī is [like] a deep ocean [of knowledge]."

—Imām al-Ḥaramayn al-Juwaynī (d. 478/1085)

"Al-Ghazālī is the second [Imām] Shāfiʿī."

—Muḥammad b. Yaḥyā l-Janzī (d. 549/1154)

"Abū Ḥāmid al-Ghazālī, the Proof of Islam (Ḥujjat al-Islām) and the Muslims, the Imām of the *imāms* of religion, [is a man] whose like eyes have not seen in eloquence and elucidation, and speech and thought, and acumen and natural ability."

—ʿAbd al-Ghāfir b. Ismāʿīl al-Fārisī (d. 529/1134)

"[He was] the Proof of Islam and Muslims, Imām of the imāms of religious sciences, one of vast knowledge, the wonder of the ages, the author of many works, and [a man] of extreme intelligence and the best of the sincere."

—Imām al-Dhahabī (d. 748/1347)

"Al-Ghazālī is without doubt the most remarkable figure in all Islam."

—T.J. DeBoer

". . . A man who stands on a level with Augustine and Luther in religious insight and intellectual vigor."

—H.A.R. Gibb

"I have to some extent found, and I believe others can find, in the words and example of al-Ghazālī a true *iḥyāʾ* . . ."

—Richard J. McCarthy, S.J.

وَإِذِ ٱعۡتَزَلۡتُمُوهُمۡ وَمَا يَعۡبُدُونَ إِلَّا ٱللَّهَ فَأۡوُۥٓاْ إِلَى ٱلۡكَهۡفِ يَنشُرۡ لَكُمۡ رَبُّكُم
مِّن رَّحۡمَتِهِۦ وَيُهَيِّئۡ لَكُم مِّنۡ أَمۡرِكُم مِّرۡفَقٗا ١٦

And when you have withdrawn from them and that which they worship other than God, retreat to the cave. Your Lord will spread out for you of His mercy and will prepare for you from your affair facility..

Sūrat al-Kahf

18:16

The Forty Books of the Revival of the Religious Sciences (*Iḥyāʾ ʿulūm al-dīn*)

The Quarter of Worship

1 The Book of Knowledge
2 The Principles of the Creed
3 The Mysteries of Purification
4 The Mysteries of the Prayer
5 The Mysteries of Charity
6 The Mysteries of Fasting
7 The Mysteries of the Pilgrimage
8 The Etiquette of the Recitation of the Qurʾān
9 Invocations and Supplications
10 The Arrangement of the Litanies and the Exposition of the Night Vigil

The Quarter of Customs

11 The Proprieties of Eating
12 The Proprieties of Marriage
13 The Proprieties of Acquisition and Earning a Living
14 The Lawful and the Unlawful
15 The Proprieties of Friendship and Brotherhood
16 **The Proprieties of Retreat**
17 The Proprieties of Travel
18 The Proprieties of the Audition and Ecstasy
19 The Commanding of Right and the Forbidding of Wrong
20 The Proprieties of Living and the Prophetic Mannerisms

The Quarter of Perils

21 The Exposition of the Wonders of the Heart
22 Training the Soul, Refining the Character, and Treating the Ailments of the Heart
23 Overcoming the Two Desires
24 The Bane of the Tongue
25 The Bane of Anger, Malice, and Envy
26 The Censure of This World
27 The Censure of Greed and the Love of Wealth
28 The Censure of Fame and Hypocritical Ostentation
29 The Censure of Pride and Vanity
30 The Censure of Deceit

The Quarter of Deliverance

31 On Repentance
32 On Patience and Thankfulness
33 On Fear and Hope
34 On Poverty and Abstinence
35 On Unity and Trust
36 On Love, Longing, Intimacy, and Contentment
37 On Intention, Sincerity, and Truthfulness
38 On Vigilance and Accounting
39 On Contemplation
40 On the Remembrance of Death and the Hereafter

THE PROPRIETIES OF RETREAT
Kitāb ādāb al-ʿuzla

Book 16 of
Iḥyāʾ ʿulūm al-dīn
The Revival of the Religious Sciences

ٱللَّهِ ٱلرَّحْمَٰنِ ٱلرَّحِيمِ

AL-GHAZĀLĪ

Kitāb ādāb al-ʿuzla

THE PROPRIETIES OF RETREAT

Book 16 of the *Iḥyāʾ ʿulūm al-dīn*

THE REVIVAL OF THE RELIGIOUS SCIENCES

Translated *by* James Pavlin

Fons Vitae
2023

The Proprieties of Retreat, Book 16 of *The Revival of the Religious Sciences* first published in 2023 by

Fons Vitae
49 Mockingbird Valley Drive
Louisville, KY 40207 USA

www.fonsvitae.com

The Fons Vitae Ghazali Series
Library of Congress Control Number: 2022952168
ISBN 978-1-94-1610-62-6

Copyediting and indexing: Valerie Joy Turner
Book design and typesetting: www.scholarlytype.com
Text typeface: Adobe Minion Pro 11/13.5

Cover art courtesy of National Library of Egypt, Cairo.
Qurʾānic frontispiece to part 19. Written and illuminated by ʿAbdallāh b. Muḥammad al-Ḥamadānī for Sultan Uljaytu 713/1313. Hamadan.

Printed in Canada

Contents

Editor's Note

This is the complete translation of *Kitāb ādāb al-ʿuzla, The Proprieties of Retreat*, book 16 of the *Iḥyāʾ ʿulūm al-dīn* of Abū Ḥāmid Muḥammad al-Ghazālī. It is a translation of the published Arabic text of volume 4 (pages 243–326), edited by Dār al-Minhāj (Jedda, 2011); the Dār al-Minhāj editors utilized additional manuscripts and early printed editions, as mentioned on pages 51–111 of the introductory volume.

Arabic terms that appear in italics follow the transliteration system of the *International Journal of Middle East Studies.* Common era (CE) dates have been added and follow Hijri dates. The blessings on prophets and others, as used by Imām al-Ghazālī, are represented in the original Arabic, as listed below.

Arabic	English	Usage
عَزَّ وَجَلَّ	Mighty and majestic is He	On mention of God
سُبْحَانَهُ وَتَعَالَىٰ	Exalted and most high is He	Used together or separately
صَلَّى ٱللَّهُ عَلَيْهِ وَسَلَّمَ	Blessings and peace of God be upon him	On mention of the Prophet Muḥammad
عَلَيْهِ ٱلسَّلَامُ	Peace be upon him	On mention of one
عَلَيْهِمُ ٱلسَّلَامُ	Peace be upon them	or more prophets
رَضِيَ ٱللَّهُ عَنْهُ	God be pleased with him	On mention of one or more
رَضِيَ ٱللَّهُ عَنْهُمْ	God be pleased with them	Companions of the Prophet
رَضِيَ ٱللَّهُ عَنْهَا	God be pleased with her	On mention of a female Companion of the Prophet
رَحِمَهُ ٱللَّهُ	God have mercy on him	On mention of someone who is deceased

This translation includes the footnotes and references provided by the editors of the Dār al-Minhāj edition. In addition, the translator has added comments from Murtaḍā l-Zabīdī's *Itḥāf* (a detailed commentary on the *Iḥyāʾ ʿulūm al-dīn*) and identified many of Imām al-Ghazālī's sources. The translator and editors have provided explanatory footnotes as necessary; editorial clarification in the text appears in hard brackets.

In addition, we have compiled a short biography of Imām al-Ghazālī with a chronology of important events in his life. This is followed by an extract from Imām al-Ghazālī's introduction to the *Iḥyāʾ ʿulūm al-dīn; it* serves as a guide to the *Revival of the Religious Sciences* for those reading Imām al-Ghazālī for the first time.

In an effort to be precise with regard to the tone and implications of Arabic words and to accurately and consistently denote their meanings in English, we have translated the following words related to retreat as *ʿuzla* (retreat), *khalwā* (seclusion), *ʿitazila* or *infirād* (isolation or withdrawal), and *tajarrud, waḥda, istīḥāsh* (isolation or solitude). The opposites of these terms are *mukhālaṭa* (socializing), *muʿāmala* (mutual interactions). Other key terms include *istiʾnās* (familiarity) and *munājat* (intimate conversations [with God]). For this edition we retained the page numbers of volume 4 of the Arabic edition in the margins after the vertical line mark |.

Biography of Imām al-Ghazālī

He is Abū Ḥāmid Muḥammad b. Muḥammad b. Muḥammad b. Aḥmad al-Ghazālī l-Ṭūsī; he was born in 450/1058 in the village of Ṭābarān near Ṭūs (in northeast Iran) and he died there, at the age of fifty-five, in 505/1111. Muḥammad's father died when he and his younger brother Aḥmad were still young; their father left a little money for their education in the care of a Sufi friend of limited means. When the money ran out, their caretaker suggested that they enroll in a *madrasa*. The *madrasa* system meant they had a stipend, room, and board. Al-Ghazālī studied *fiqh* in his hometown under a Sufi named Aḥmad al-Rādhakānī; he then traveled to Jurjān and studied under Ismāʿīl b. Masʿada al-Ismāʿīlī (d. 477/1084).

On his journey home his caravan was overtaken by highway robbers who took all of their possessions. Al-Ghazālī went to the leader of the bandits and demanded his notebooks. The leader asked, what are these notebooks? Al-Ghazālī answered: "This is the knowledge that I traveled far to acquire," the leader acquiesced to al-Ghazālī's demands after stating: "If you claim that it is knowledge that you have, how can we take it away from you?" This incident left a lasting impression on the young scholar. Thereafter, he returned to Ṭūs for three years, where he committed to memory all that he had learned thus far.

In 469/1077 he traveled to Nīshāpūr to study with the leading scholar of his time, Imām al-Ḥaramayn al-Juwaynī (d. 478/1085), at the Niẓāmiyya College; al-Ghazālī remained his student for approximately eight years, until al-Juwaynī died. Al-Ghazālī was one of his most illustrious students, and al-Juwaynī referred to him as "a deep ocean [of knowledge]." As one of al-Juwaynī star pupils, al-Ghazālī used to fill in as a substitute lecturer in his teacher's absence. He also tutored his fellow students in the subjects that al-Juwaynī taught at the Niẓāmiyya. Al-Ghazālī wrote his first book, on the founding principles of legal theory (*uṣūl al-fiqh*), while studying with al-Juwaynī.

Very little is known about al-Ghazālī's family, though some biographers mention that he married while in Nīshāpūr; others note that he had married in Ṭūs prior to leaving for Nīshāpūr. Some accounts state that he had five children, a son who died early and four daughters. Accounts also indicate that his mother lived to see her son rise to fame and fortune.

After the death of al-Juwaynī, al-Ghazālī went to the camp (*al-muʿaskar*) of the Saljūq *wazīr* Niẓām al-Mulk (d. 485/1192). He stayed at the camp, which was a gathering place for scholars, and quickly distinguished himself among their illustrious company. Niẓām al-Mulk recognized al-Ghazālī's genius and appointed him professor at the famed Niẓāmiyya College of Baghdad.

Al-Ghazālī left for Baghdad in 484/1091 and stayed there four years—it was a very exciting time to be in the heart of the Islamic empire. At the Niẓāmiyya College he had many students, by some estimates as many as three hundred. In terms of his scholarly output, this was also a prolific period in which he wrote *Maqāṣid al-falāsifa*, *Tahāfut al-falāsifa*, *al-Mustaẓhirī,* and other works.

Al-Ghazālī was well-connected politically and socially; we have evidence that he settled disputes related to the legitimacy of the rule of the ʿAbbāsid caliph, al-Mustaẓhir (r. 487–512/1094–1118) who assumed his role as the caliph when he was just fifteen years old, after the death of his father al-Muqtadī (d. 487/1094). Al-Ghazālī issued a *fatwā* of approval of the appointment of al-Mustaẓhir and was present at the oath-taking ceremony.

In Baghdad, al-Ghazālī underwent a spiritual crisis, during which he was overcome by fear of the punishment of the hellfire. He became convinced that he was destined for the hellfire if he did not change his ways; he feared that he had become too engrossed in worldly affairs, to the detriment of his spiritual being. He began to question his true intentions: was he writing and teaching to serve God, or because he enjoyed the fame and fortune that resulted from his lectures. He experienced much suffering, both inward and outward; one day as he stood before his students to present a lecture, he found himself unable to speak. The physicians were unable to diagnose any physical malady. Al-Ghazālī remained in Baghdad for a time, then left his teaching post for the pilgrimage. He left behind fortune, fame, and influence. He was beloved by his numerous students and had many admirers, including the sultan; he was also envied by many. The presumption is that he left in the manner he did—ostensibly to undertake the pilgrimage—because if he had made public his intentions to leave permanently, those around him would have tried to convince him to remain and the temptation might have been too strong to resist.

After leaving Baghdad, he changed direction and headed toward Damascus; according to his autobiography he disappeared from the intellectual scene for ten years. This does not mean that he did not teach, but that he did not want to return to public life and be paid for teaching. This ten-year period can be divided into two phases. First, he spent two years in the East—in greater Syria and on the pilgrimage. We have evidence that while on his return to Ṭūs he appeared at a Sufi lodge opposite the Niẓāmiyya College in Baghdad. He spent the second phase of the ten-year period (the remaining eight years) in Ṭūs, where he wrote the famed *Iḥyāʾ ʿulūm al-dīn*, a work that was inspired by the change in his outlook that resulted from his spiritual crisis.

When he arrived back in his hometown in 490/1097, he established a school and a Sufi lodge, in order to continue teaching and learning. In 499/1106, Niẓām al-Mulk's son, Fakhr al-Mulk, requested that al-Ghazālī accept a teaching position at his old school, the Niẓāmiyya of Nīshāpūr. He accepted and taught for a time, but left this position in 500/1106 after Fakhr al-Mulk was assassinated by Ismāʿīlīs. He then returned to Ṭūs and divided his time between teaching and worship. He died in 505/1111 and was buried in a cemetery near the citadel of Ṭābarān.

Legacy and Contributions of al-Ghazālī

Al-Ghazālī's two hundred and seventy-three works span many disciplines and can be grouped under the following headings:

1. Jurisprudence and legal theory. Al-Ghazālī made foundational contributions to Shāfiʿī jurisprudence; his book *al-Wajīz* is major handbook that has been used in teaching institutions around the world; many commentaries have been written on it, most notably by Abū l-Qāsim ʿAbd al-Karīm al-Rāfiʿī (d. 623/1226). In legal theory, *al-Mustaṣfa min ʿilm al-uṣūl* is considered one of five foundational texts in the discipline.
2. Logic and philosophy. Al-Ghazālī introduced logic in Islamic terms that jurists could understand and utilize. His works on philosophy include the *Tahāfut al-falāsifa*, which has been studied far beyond the Muslim world and has been the subject of numerous commentaries, discussions, and refutations.
3. Theology, including works on heresiography in refutation of Bāṭinī doctrines. He also expounded on the theory of occasionalism.
4. Ethics and educational theory. The *Mīzān al-ʿamal* and other works such as the *Iḥyāʾ ʿulūm al-dīn* mention a great deal on education.
5. Spirituality and Sufism. His magnum opus, the *Iḥyāʾ ʿulūm al-dīn* is a pioneering work in the field of spirituality, in terms of its organization and its comprehensive scope.
6. Various fields. Al-Ghazālī also wrote shorter works in a variety of disciplines, including his autobiography (*al-Munqidh min al-ḍalāl*), works on Qurʾānic studies (*Jawāhir al-Qurʾān*), and political statecraft (*Naṣiḥat al-mūluk*).

Chronology of al-Ghazālī's Life

450/1058	Birth of al-Ghazālī at Ṭūs
c. 461/1069	Began studies at Ṭūs
c. 465/1073	Traveled to Jurjān to study
466–469/1074–1077	Studied at Ṭūs
469/1077	Studied with al-Jūwaynī at the Niẓāmiyya college in Nīshāpūr
473/1080	al-Ghazālī composed his first book, *al-Mankhūl fī l-uṣūl*
477/1084	Death of al-Fāramdhī, one of al-Ghazālī's teachers
25 Rabīʿ II 478/ 20 August 1085	Death of al-Jūwaynī; al-Ghazālī left Nīshāpūr
Jumāda I 484/ July 1091	Appointed to teach at the Niẓāmiyya college in Baghdad
10 Ramaḍān 485/ 14 October 1092	Niẓām-al-Mulk was assassinated
484–487/1091–1094	Studied philosophy
Muḥarrām 487/ February 1094	Attended the oath-taking of the new caliph, al-Mustaẓhir
487/1094	Finished *Maqāṣid al-falāsifa*
5 Muḥarrām 488/ 21 January 1095	Finished *Tahāfut al-falāsifa*
Rajab 488/ July 1095	Experienced a spiritual crisis
Dhū l-Qaʿda 488/ November 1095	Left Baghdad for Damascus
Dhū l-Qaʿda 489/ November – December 1096	Made pilgrimage and worked on the *Iḥyāʾ ʿulūm al-dīn*
Jumāda II 490/ May 1097	Taught from the *Iḥyāʾ ʿulūm al-dīn* during a brief stop in Baghdad
Rajab 490/June 1097	Seen in Baghdad by Abū Bakr b. al-ʿArabī
Fall 490/1097	Returned to Ṭūs

Dhū l-Ḥijja 490/ November 1097	Established a *madrasa* and a *khānqāh* in Ṭūs
Dhū l-Qaʿda 499/ July 1106	Taught at the Niẓāmiyya college in Nīshāpūr
500/1106	Wrote *al-Munqidh min al-ḍalāl*
500/1106	Returned to Ṭūs
28 Dhū l-Ḥijja 502/ 5 August 1109	Finished *al-Mustaṣfā min ʿilm al-uṣūl*
Jumada I 505/ December 1111	Finished *Iljām al-ʿawām ʿan ʿilm al-kalām*
14 Jumada II 505/ 18 December 1111	Imām al-Ghazālī died in Ṭūs

Eulogies in Verse

Because of him the lame walked briskly,
And the songless through him burst into melody.

On the death of Imām al-Ghazālī, Abū l-Muẓaffar Muḥammad al-Abiwardī said of his loss:

He is gone! and the greatest loss which ever afflicted me,
was that of a man who left no one like him among mankind.

About the *Revival of the Religious Sciences*

THE present work is book 16 of Imām al-Ghazālī's forty-volume masterpiece. Below is an excerpt from al-Ghazālī's introduction that explains the arrangement and purpose of the *Iḥyāʾ ʿulūm al-dīn.*

People have composed books concerning some of these ideas, but this book [the *Iḥyāʾ*] differs from them in five ways, by

1. clarifying what they have obscured and elucidating what they have treated casually;
2. arranging what they scattered and putting in order what they separated;
3. abbreviating what they made lengthy and proving what they reported;
4. omitting what they have repeated; and
5. establishing the truth of certain obscure matters that are difficult to understand and which have not been presented in books at all.

For although all the scholars follow one course, there is no reason one should not proceed independently and bring to light something unknown, paying special attention to something his colleagues have forgotten. Or they are not heedless about calling attention to it, but they neglect to mention it in books. Or they do not overlook it, but something prevents them from exposing it [and making it clear].

So these are the special properties of this book, besides its inclusion of all these various kinds of knowledge.

Two things induced me to arrange this book in four parts. The first and fundamental motive is that this arrangement in establishing what is true and in making it understandable is, as it were, inevitable because the branch of knowledge by which one approaches the hereafter is divided into the knowledge of [proper] conduct and the knowledge of [spiritual] unveiling.

By the knowledge of [spiritual] unveiling I mean knowledge and only knowledge. By the science of [proper] conduct I mean knowledge as well as action in accordance with that knowledge. This work will deal only with the science of [proper] conduct, and not with [spiritual] unveiling, which one is not permitted to record in writing, although it is the ultimate aim of saints and the ultimate aim of the sincere. The science of [proper] conduct is merely a path that leads to unveiling and only through that path did the prophets of God communicate with the people and lead them to Him. Concerning [spiritual] unveiling, the prophets عَلَيْهِمُ السَّلَامُ spoke only figuratively and briefly through signs and symbols, because they realized the inability of people's minds to comprehend. Therefore since the scholars are heirs of the prophets, they cannot but follow in their footsteps and emulate their way.

The knowledge of [proper] conduct is divided into (1) outward knowledge, by which I mean knowledge of the senses and (2) inward knowledge, by which I mean knowledge of the functions of the heart.

The physical members either perform acts of prescribed worship, or acts that are in accordance with custom, while the heart, because it is removed from the senses and belongs to the world of dominion, is subject to either praiseworthy or blameworthy [influences]. Therefore it is necessary to divide this branch of knowledge into two parts: outward and inward. The outward part, which is connected to the senses, is subdivided into acts of worship and acts that pertain to custom. The inward part, which is connected to the states of the heart and the characteristics of the soul, is subdivided into blameworthy states and praiseworthy states. So the total makes four divisions of the sciences of the practice of religion.

The second motive [for this division] is that I have noticed the sincere interest of students in jurisprudence, which has become popular among those who do not fear God تَعَالَىٰ but who seek to boast and exploit its influence and prestige in arguments. It [jurisprudence] is also divided into four quarters, and he who follows the style of one who is beloved becomes beloved.

Translator's Introduction

This translation of al-Ghazālī's *Kitāb ādāb al-ʿuzla* (*The Book on the Proprieties of Retreat*) addresses retreat, one of the many topics that comprise al-Ghazālī's monumental work known as the *Iḥyāʾ ʿulūm al-dīn* (*Revival of the Religious Sciences*). As indicated by its title, the main discussion in book 16 is the question of whether one should engage in socializing (*mukhālaṭa*) or retreat from society to devote oneself to strengthening one's relationship with God. Al-Ghazālī takes us through the benefits and dangers of retreat, while laying out guidelines for those who choose it. Far from being an arcane topic for scholarly debate, in fact it is highly relevant for those who seek the safe return to their Lord in the hereafter.

Al-Ghazālī delves into the human psyche to explain the behavior of his fellow Muslims. For example, he presents the case of someone who may be motivated to go into retreat out of a sense of arrogance or conceit, or in an attempt to prompt people to praise him for his piety. This would negate the purpose of retreat and bring that person spiritual ruin.

In preparing this translation, it was necessary to pay close attention to the Arabic text as well as the overall Islamic context of al-Ghazālī's writings and the specific historical circumstances in which he lived. The Arabic is eloquent and rich, yet quite concise; his mastery of the language was and remains impressive. Writing the *Iḥyāʾ* at the end of the fifth century AH/eleventh century CE, he was able to draw on a rich literature that included information about the Prophet ﷺ, his Companions, their students (known as the Followers), and several generations of scholars, historians, ascetics, and poets. A glimpse into this literature can be seen in the footnotes provided by the editors of the Dār al-Minhāj edition, which was used for this translation. By al-Ghazālī's time, much of this vast array of information had already been collected into works that circulated widely throughout the great intellectual centers of the Islamic world, stretching from North Africa to Central Asia. Baghdad, the seat of the ʿAbbāsid caliphate where al-Ghazālī lived and taught, was at the center of this Islamic civilization.

In order to produce a readable English translation that conveys the meaning and context of al-Ghazālī's book on retreat, I depended on secondary sources that elaborate his ideas. To this end, I am indebted to Murtaḍā al-Zabīdī's well-known commentary, *Itḥāf al-sādat al-muttaqīn bi-sharḥ Iḥyāʾ ʿulūm al-dīn*, on the *Iḥyāʾ*. Al-Zabīdī mastered the Arabic language, as evidenced by his 40-volume Arabic dictionary known as *Tāj al-ʿarūs*, an extensive commentary on al-Fīrūzābādī's *al-Qāmūs al-muḥīṭ* (an eighth-/fourteenth-century dictionary). Al-Zabīdī was also a scholar of *ḥadīth* (a *muḥaddith*), which enabled him to give extensive details on the narrations in the *Iḥyāʾ* that are traced back to the Prophet صَلَّى ٱللَّٰهُ عَلَيْهِ وَسَلَّمَ, the Companions, the Followers, and other prominent figures that cross the pages of the *Iḥyāʾ*. Al-Zabīdī himself made use of an earlier work that identifies the authenticity of the *ḥadīth*s in the *Iḥyāʾ*. This was a work by the *ḥadīth* scholar al-ʿIrāqī (d. 807/1404 or 1405) called *al-Mughnī ʿan ḥaml al-asfār fī takhrīj mā fī l-iḥyāʾ min al-akhbār*.

Among the sources al-Ghazālī cites are the well-known *ḥadīth* collections, poetry (*dīwāns*), and historical annals. The six *ḥadīth* collections are those of al-Bukhārī (d. 256/870), Muslim (d. 261/874 or 875), Ibn Mājah (d. 273/866 or 867), Abū Dāwūd (d. 275/888 or 889), al-Tirmidhī (d. 279/892 or 893), and al-Nasāʾī (d. 303/915 or 916). I provided the death dates of other authors, in an effort to give some historical context to the literature.

THE PROPRIETIES OF RETREAT

Kitāb ādāb al-ʿuzla

the Sixth Book of

the Quarter of

Customs

Book 16

of the *Revival of*

the Religious Sciences

245

[al-Ghazālī's Introduction]

The Book of the Proprieties of Retreat

In the Name of God, the Merciful and Compassionate

All praise to God, who magnified the blessings on the best of His creation and His elect, by directing their concern to familiarity with [the remembrance of God]. [God] increased their lot of delight in witnessing His signs and grandeur and calmed their hearts with His intimate exchanges (*munājāt*) and His kindness. He decreased their concern for the pleasure and beauty of this world in their hearts, so each became content with retreat when the veils were lifted from the flow of their contemplation [of God]. Thus, he [whose veils were lifted] became familiar in his seclusion (*khalwā*) with witnessing the splendor of [God's] سُبۡحَانَهُۥ وَتَعَالَىٰ countenance. He [felt] an aversion to familiarity with friends even if they were among his closest companions.

Blessings be on our master Muḥammad, the master of His prophets and His chosen one, and on his family and his Companions who are the masters and leaders of all people.[1]

To proceed, indeed people differ greatly [in their views] about retreat (*ʿuzla*) and socializing (*mukhālaṭa*), and the preference for one over the other. Each one of [the two] has [aspects of] danger that are inseparable and repel [people] and [each one also has aspects that] bring benefit. |

The inclination of most of the worshipers and ascetics is to 246
choose retreat and favor it over socializing. In the previous book on

1 Another manuscript of the *Iḥyāʾ ʿulūm al-dīn* has truth (*ḥaqq*) instead of people (*khalq*).

friendship,[2] we mentioned the virtues of socializing, brotherhood, and friendship, all of which almost contradict the inclination of many to choose isolation (*istīḥāsh*) and seclusion (*khalwā*). So unveiling the truth of this matter is important. This outline can be achieved in two chapters. Chapter 1: On the transmission of opinions and giving evidence for [retreat] and chapter 2: On unveiling the truth by defining the benefits and dangers [of retreat].

2 This is a reference to *Kitāb ādāb al-ṣuḥba wa-l-maʿāshara maʿ aṣnāf al-khalaq* [*The Proprieties of Friendship and Brotherhood*], book 15 of the *Revival of the Religious Sciences.*

1

On the Transmission of the Opinions and Statements and the Evidence of the Two Groups on the Matter [of Retreat]

People have different opinions [on this matter], and their differences were apparent among the Followers (*tābiʿīn*).[1] Those who chose retreat (*ʿuzla*) and favored it over socializing included Sufyān al-Thawrī, Ibrāhīm b. Adham, Dāwūd al-Ṭāʾī, [al-] Fuḍayl b. ʿIyāḍ, Sulaymān al-Khawwāṣ, Yūsuf b. Asbāṭ, Ḥudhayfa al-Marʿashī, and Bishr [b. al-Ḥārith] al-Ḥāfī.[2]

Most of the Followers preferred socializing and sought to increase [their] acquaintances and brothers in order to form bonds with, and show affection for, the believers. This aided them in the *dīn*[3] and encouraged righteousness and piety. Those who were inclined toward this view were Saʿīd b. al-Musayyab, al-Shaʿbī, Ibn Abī Laylā, Hishām b. ʿUrwa, Ibn Shubrama, Shurayḥ [al-Qāḍī], Sharīk b. ʿAbdallāh [b. Abī ʿUmar], [Sufyān] Ibn ʿUyayna [al-Kūfī], Ibn al-Mubārak, al-Shāfiʿī, Aḥmad b. Ḥanbal, and many more.[4] |

1 The second generation of the Prophet's Followers (*tābiʿīn*).

2 Trans. note: al-Zabīdī, writes "These people were not from the generation of the Followers. It is only that their view agreed with the view of the Followers." Al-Zabīdī, *Itḥāf*, 6:330. This also applies to the names mentioned in the next paragraph.

3 *Dīn*, often translated as "religion," more accurately means a way of life based on belief, devotion, and virtue.

4 Abū Ṭālib al-Makkī, *Qūt al-qulūb*, 2:214. In his commentary on the *Iḥyāʾ*, al-Zabīdī lists several statements regarding the preference for retreat or socializing. Then [al-Zabīdī] writes "Al-Kirmānī [d. 786/1384] said in *Sharḥ al-Bukhārī*, 'In our time, we

248 The statements from the scholars can be divided into general statements, indicating an inclination for one of the two opinions, and statements that relate to the reason for [their] inclination. We now bring the general points of these statements and explain the opinions concerning them. We present what refers to the reasons [for the scholars'] inclinations by exposing the dangers and benefits [of retreat and socializing]. So we mention [the following].

It has been reported from ʿUmar [b. al-Khaṭṭāb] رَضِيَ اللَّهُ عَنْهُ that he said, "Take your share of retreat."[5]

Ibn Sīrīn said, "Retreat is worship."[6]

Al-Fuḍayl [b. ʿIyāḍ] said, "Let God be sufficient as a lover, the Qurʾān as a comforting friend (*muʾnis*), and death as an admonisher. Take God as a companion, and leave people to the side."[7]

The ascetic Abū l-Rabīʿ said to Dāwūd al-Ṭāʾī, "Admonish me!" He said, "Fast from this world and make the hereafter the end of your fast, and flee from people as you would flee from a lion."[8]

Ḥasan [b. ʿAlī] رَضِيَ اللَّهُ عَنْهُمَا said,

> Here are some statements I memorized from the Torah: A contented person (*ibn ādam*) is free, [a person who] withdraws from people is safe, [a person who] abandons desire is free of need (*istaghnā*), [a person who] abandons envy |
> 249 manifests his valor (*murūʿa*), [a person who] is a little patient has prolonged enjoyment.[9]

---

choose to prefer retreat because we turn toward the assemblies free of disobedience.' Al-Badr al-ʿAynī [d. 855/1451] said, 'I agree with him in what he said. Socializing with people in this time brings only evil.' Abū l-Baqāʾ al-Aḥmadī said, 'I say that the virtue of retreat lies in its removal of ostentation in actions, its freeing of the mind, and its witnessing the secret of [God's] oneness in eternity.' I [al-Zabīdī] agree with what they have said about the preference for retreat because of the corruption of the time and the brothers. Help is sought only with God." Al-Zabīdī, *Itḥāf*, 6:331.

5 Ibn al-Mubārak (d. 181/797), *al-Zuhd*, 11, from the addendum of narrations of Naʿīm b. Ḥammād and by Ibn Ḥibbān (d. 354/965), *Rawḍat al-ʿuqalāʾ*, 81.

6 Al-Khaṭṭābī (d. 388/998), *al-ʿUzla*, 27.

7 Al-Khaṭṭābī, *al-ʿUzla*, 33, [with the first sentence only]. The second sentence, "Take God as a companion…," was reported by Abū Nuʿaym (d. 430/1038 or 1039), *Ḥilya*, 7:373 from Ibrāhīm b. Adham (d. 165/782), who recited this while working.

8 Al-Khaṭṭābī, *al-ʿUzla*, 34; al-Qushayrī (d. 465/1072 or 1073), *al-Risāla*, 60.

9 Al-Khaṭṭābī, *al-ʿUzla*, 37. There is evidence in the traditions that these five statements can be attributed to the Prophet صَلَّى اللَّهُ عَلَيْهِ وَسَلَّمَ. Al-Zabīdī, *Itḥāf*, 6:332.

Wuhayb b. al-Ward said, "It has reached us that wisdom is comprised of ten parts. Nine of them are in silence, and the tenth part is in retreat from people."[10]

Yūsuf b. Muslim said to ʿAlī b. Bakkār, "What compels you to stay alone?" He had been keeping himself confined to the house. He said, "When I was a young man I was patient with something more difficult than this. I sat with people and did not talk to them."[11]

Sufyān al-Thawrī said, "This is the time for silence and confinement to houses."[12]

One of them said,

> I was on a ship, and one of the young men of the ʿAlawiyya[13] was with us. Seven days passed without us hearing anything from him.
>
> We said, "What is this? God has brought us together for seven days, but we have not seen you converse with us or speak to us."

Then he recited this [poetry],[14]

> Of little distress, no child dies
> And no affair one guards against but it passes away |
>
> The needs of youth are fulfilled, and one benefits only as to knowledge 250
> Then the ultimate limit of it is to be solitary and silent

Ibrāhīm al-Nakhaʿī said to a man, "Study, then seclude yourself." Al-Rabīʿ b. Khuthaym mentioned this.[15]

It is said that Mālik b. Anas used to attend funerals, visit the sick, and give brothers their rights. Then he abandoned these [actions]

---

10 Al-Khaṭṭābī, *al-ʿUzla*, 38; Abū Nuʿaym, *Ḥilya*, 8:142; Ibn ʿAdī, *al-Kāmil*, 6:442, as attributed to the Prophet صَلَّى ٱللَّهُ عَلَيْهِ وَسَلَّمَ.

11 Al-Khaṭṭābī, *al-ʿUzla*, 39.

12 Al-Khaṭṭābī, *al-ʿUzla*, 40.

13 This refers to a descendant of ʿAlī b. Abī Ṭālib رَضِيَ ٱللَّهُ عَنْهُ (d. 40/660 or 661). Al-Zabīdī, *Itḥāf*, 6:332.

14 Al-Khaṭṭābī, *al-ʿUzla*, 40; from Muḥammad b. Yūsuf al-Naḥwī, from one of his shaykhs. Ibn Abī l-Ḥadīd, *Sharḥ nahj al-balāgha*, 10:40–41.

15 Al-Khaṭṭābī, *al-ʿUzla*, 42; Ibrāhīm al-Nakhaʿī and al-Rabīʿ b. Khuthaym transmitted this through two different chains of narrators.

one by one until he abandoned all of them. He used to say, "A man need not inform [people] of all his excuses."[16]

It was said to ʿUmar b. ʿAbd al-ʿAzīz, "If only you had some free time for us." He said, "Free time has departed. There is no free time except with God تَعَالَىٰ."[17]

Al-Fuḍayl [b. ʿIyāḍ] said, "Indeed, I have a favor [to ask] of men [i.e., other people]: when he meets me, he does not greet me, and when I am sick, he does not visit me."[18]

Abū Sulaymān al-Dārānī said,

> While al-Rabīʿ b. Khuthaym was sitting at the door to his house, it so happened that a stone struck him on the cheek, causing him to bleed. He wiped the blood, and said to [to himself], "You have been admonished, O Rabīʿ!" Then he got up and went into his home. After that, he never sat at the door to his home until he was brought out for his funeral.[19] |

251 Saʿd b. Abī Waqqāṣ and Saʿīd b. Zayd used to stay in their homes in al-ʿAqīq. They did not go to Medina for the Friday congregational prayer or for any other reason until they died in al-ʿAqīq.[20]

Yūsuf b. Asbāṭ said that he heard Sufyān al-Thawrī say, "By God, there is no god but He. Retreat is certainly allowable."[21]

---

16 Al-Khaṭṭābī, *al-ʿUzla*, 50. Mālik b. Anas (d. 179/795) remained in retreat for almost twelve years. The people of his time came to dislike this from him and there was much talk about him. Al-Zabīdī, *Itḥāf*, 6:333.

17 Ibn Saʿd (d. 230/844 or 845), *Ṭabaqāt*, 7:385.

18 Trans. note: al-Zabīdī mentions that it is reported by Abū Nuʿaym in *Ḥilya*. Al-Zabīdī, *Itḥāf*, 6:333.

19 Ibn al-Jawzī (d. 597/1200 or 1201), *Ṣifat al-ṣafwa*, 3:33.

20 Ibn Abī l-Dunyā (d. 281/894 or 895), *al-ʿUzla wa-l-infirād*, 58. The original report is in Mālik, *al-Muwaṭṭaʾ*, 1:232. Trans. note: al-ʿAqīq is about ten miles outside Medina. When these two Companions of the Prophet صَلَّى ٱللَّٰهُ عَلَيْهِ وَسَلَّمَ died, they were brought to Medina for burial in the cemetery of al-Baqīʿ. Saʿīd died in 51/671, and Saʿd died in 55/674. Al-Zabīdī, *Itḥāf*, 6:333.

21 Abū Nuʿaym, *Ḥilya*, 6:288. Al-Yāfiʿī (d. 768/1366 or 1367), *al-Irshād wa-l-taṭrīz*, 133, transmitted this statement from a gnostic, "If it was allowable during his time, then it is obligatory during our time."

Bishr b. ʿAbdallāh said, "Limit your association with people. You do not know what it will be like on the day of resurrection. Thus, if you are put to shame, very few will know you."[22]

One of the governors came to Ḥātim al-Aṣamm and said to him, "Do you need anything?" He said, "Yes." He asked, "What is it?" He said, "That you do not see me, and I do not see you."

A man said to Sahl [al-Tustarī], "I want to be your companion." He said, "When one of us has died, who will be his companion in the hereafter. Thus let him be his companion now."[23] |

It was said to al-Fuḍayl [b. ʿIyāḍ], 252

> Your son, ʿAlī, says, "I would love to be in a place from which I can see people but they cannot see me." Al-Fuḍayl began to cry and said, "O woe to you ʿAlī! Why have you not perfected it?"
>
> Then he said, "I do not see them, and they do not see me."[24]

Al-Fuḍayl also said, "Having many acquaintances is a sign of weakness in a man's intellect."[25]

Ibn ʿAbbās رَضِيَ اللَّهُ عَنْهُمَا said, "The most virtuous assembly is the gathering inside your house where you do not see [anyone] and are not seen."[26]

These are the statements of those inclined toward retreat. |

---

22 Ibn Abī l-Dunyā, *al-ʿUzla wa-l-infirād*, 102; Abū Nuʿaym, *Ḥilya*, 6:241, from Bishr b. Manṣūr al-Salamī.

23 Edition A states "then he is his companion, so let him be his companion now." Edition B states "then who will be his companion going to the hereafter. Thus let him be his companion now." The report was transmitted by al-Qushayrī, *al-Risāla*, 487, with this wording, "When one of us has died, then who will be the companion of the one remaining? He said, 'God.' Thus he said to him, 'Then let Him be his companion now.'" Al-Zabīdī writes, "This indicates the soundness of allowing companionship with God. It is affirmed by the narration, 'O God, You are my companion on the journey.'" Al-Zabīdī, *Itḥāf*, 6:334. Trans. note: For the *ḥadīth* "O God, You are...," see Muslim, *Ṣaḥīḥ*, 1342, and al-Tirmidhī, *Sunan*, 3447.

24 Al-Zabīdī said, "Abū Nuʿaym extracted it from *Ḥilya*. It indicates that the second station is a more virtuous rank than the first because his seeing people is a great distraction from God سُبْحَانَهُ وَتَعَالَى." Al-Zabīdī, *Itḥāf*, 6:334.

25 Ibn Abī l-Dunyā reported something similar in *al-ʿUzla wa-l-infirād*, 138, as a statement of Ibn Masʿūd رَضِيَ اللَّهُ عَنْهُ.

26 Al-Zabīdī attributes it to Abū Nuʿaym in *Ḥilya*. Al-Zabīdī, *Itḥāf*, 6:334.

253 **Mentioning the Evidence of Those Inclined Toward Socializing and the Weakness [of the Evidence]**

These people argue by way of these two statements of [God] تَعَالَىٰ, *And do not be like the ones who became divided and differed…* [Q. 3:105], and by His تَعَالَىٰ statement: *He brought your hearts together…* [Q. 3:103]. [God] favored people by way of bringing [hearts] together.

This [argument] is weak because what is intended is divided opinions and differing schools of thought regarding the meaning of God's Book and the principles of the law (*sharīʿa*). The purpose of friendship (*ulfa*) is to remove every type of wickedness from [people's] breasts. This [wickedness] is [among] the reasons that incite discord and lead to feuds. And retreat does not negate [the benefits of friendship].

They also argue by using the statement of the Messenger of God صَلَّىٰ ٱللَّٰهُ عَلَيْهِ وَسَلَّمَ, "The believer is the one who is friendly and is taken as a friend (*al-muʾmin ilf maʾlūf*). There is no good in the one who makes no friends and is not taken as a friend."[27]

This is another weak [argument] because [the statement only] indicates that the blameworthiness of an ill-natured [person] prevents friendship. Having a beautiful disposition is not included in [the meaning of this statement], for if the one with [a beautiful disposition] is sociable, he makes friends and is befriended. But he can avoid socializing out of concern for himself and seeking safety from others.

They argue further with this statement of the Messenger of God صَلَّىٰ ٱللَّٰهُ عَلَيْهِ وَسَلَّمَ,

> "Whoever separates from the congregation (*jamāʿa*) by a handspan has removed the rope of Islam [to which one clings] from his neck."[28] |

---

27 Ibn Ḥanbal (d. 241/855 or 856), *Musnad*, 9:134 [no. 9170]; al-Ṭabarānī (d. 360/971), *al-Muʿjam al-kabīr*, 6:131 [no. 5744]; and al-Ḥākim al-Nīsābūrī (d. 405/1014 or 1015), *al-Mustadrak*, 1:23.

28 Al-Bayhaqī (d. 458/1066), *al-Sunan al-kubrā*, 8:157. Trans. note: see also Abū Dāwūd, *Sunan*, 4758 and Ibn Ḥanbal, *Musnad*, 16:23 [no. 21453]. This is a well-known *ḥadīth* transmitted in numerous collections with slightly different wording. Al-Zabīdī, *Itḥāf*, 6:334. Two examples are included in this paragraph.

> He صَلَّى ٱللَّهُ عَلَيْهِ وَسَلَّمَ also said, "If someone separates from the congregation and dies, then his death is [like a death in the time of] ignorance (*jāhiliyya*)."[29] 254
>
> And there is his statement صَلَّى ٱللَّهُ عَلَيْهِ وَسَلَّمَ, "If someone breaks the staff of the Muslims while the Muslims are united in Islam, then he has removed the rope of Islam from his neck."[30]

This [argument] is weak because [the term] congregation (*jamāʿa*) means agreeing with the opinions [of the majority] on the leader to whom to pledge loyalty. And departing from [the opinions of the majority] is a transgression. And opposition to the [united] opinion [on the leader] and departure from [their opinions] are prohibited. It is necessary for people to follow an obeyed leader uniting their opinion. This [can] only happen with a pledge of loyalty by the majority. Opposition will spread sedition through tribulation. There is nothing in this that opposes to retreat.

[Yet again,] they argue by using the prohibition of [the Messenger of God] صَلَّى ٱللَّهُ عَلَيْهِ وَسَلَّمَ about abandoning [a Muslim] for more than three [days],

> "Whoever abandons his brother for more than three [days] and then dies will enter the fire."[31]
>
> He صَلَّى ٱللَّهُ عَلَيْهِ وَسَلَّمَ said, "It is not allowed for a Muslim to abandon his brother for more than three [days]. The one who is first [to end the separation] enters paradise."[32]

---

29 ʿAbd al-Razzāq (d. 211/826 or 827), *al-Muṣannaf* [no. 20707].

30 Al-Ṭabarānī, *al-Muʿjam al-kabīr*, 11:25 [no. 10925].

31 Abū Dāwud, *Sunan*, 4914.

32 Al-Bukhārī, *Ṣaḥīḥ*, 6065, and Muslim, *Ṣaḥīḥ*, 2558, without the addition of the last sentence [i.e., "The one who is first…"]. It is also reported by al-Ṭabarānī, *al-Muʿjam al-awsaṭ*, 7870, with this added sentence, "Whoever initiates the greeting of peace will be first into paradise." Trans. note: The full *ḥadīth* in al-Bukhārī is "Do not hate one another, and do not be jealous of one another, and do not desert each other. O worshipers of God! Be brothers. It is not permissible for any Muslim to avoid his brother for more than three days." The *ḥadīth* in Muslim is similar to this.

And he صَلَّىٱللَّهُعَلَيْهِوَسَلَّمَ said, "Whoever abandons his brother for a year is like one who has shed his blood."[33] They say that retreat is complete abandonment. |

255 This [argument] is weak because what is intended is being angry with people and persistently cutting off speech, greetings, and regular socializing [with them]. [These statements] do not include abandoning socializing [for a reason] other than anger. Moreover, abandoning [a Muslim] for more than three [days] is allowable in two circumstances. The first is when one perceives some good in continuing the abandonment [beyond three days]. The second is when one perceives himself to be safer [because of this abandonment].

The prohibition is general and applies to everything except the two circumstances [above]. The evidence for this is what was reported from ʿĀʾisha رَضِيَٱللَّهُعَنْهَا that the Prophet صَلَّىٱللَّهُعَلَيْهِوَسَلَّمَ avoided [Zaynab رَضِيَٱللَّهُعَنْهَا] for [the months of] Dhū l-Ḥijja, Muḥarram, and some of Ṣafar.[34]

ʿUmar [b. al-Khaṭṭāb] reported that [the Prophet] صَلَّىٱللَّهُعَلَيْهِوَسَلَّمَ separated from his wives and took an oath [to keep away] from them for one month. He ascended to his room, a small [upper] chamber, and stayed there for twenty-nine days, then when he descended, it was said to him, "You have been there for twenty-nine days." He said, "A month could be twenty-nine days."[35] |

---

33 Reported by Abū Dāwūd, *Sunan*, 4915, but with the statement "...is like the shedding of his blood" instead of "...is like the one who has shed his blood."

34 The avoidance mentioned here actually refers to the mother of the believers, Zaynab رَضِيَٱللَّهُعَنْهَا, when the Prophet صَلَّىٱللَّهُعَلَيْهِوَسَلَّمَ requested that she give a spare camel to Ṣafiya رَضِيَٱللَّهُعَنْهَا, whose camel had become weak. Zaynab رَضِيَٱللَّهُعَنْهَا said, "Am I to give it to that Jewess?" The Prophet صَلَّىٱللَّهُعَلَيْهِوَسَلَّمَ became angry and avoided her. ʿĀʾisha رَضِيَٱللَّهُعَنْهَا transmitted the *ḥadīth*, with the pronoun "her" in the statement "avoided her" in reference to Zaynab رَضِيَٱللَّهُعَنْهَا, not ʿĀʾisha رَضِيَٱللَّهُعَنْهَا. See Abū Dāwūd, *Sunan*, 4602. Trans. note: Ṣafiya was a Jewish woman who converted to Islam and was married to the Prophet صَلَّىٱللَّهُعَلَيْهِوَسَلَّمَ. The Prophet wanted to teach Zaynab رَضِيَٱللَّهُعَنْهَا, an upper-class Qurayshī woman, not to call Ṣafiya رَضِيَٱللَّهُعَنْهَا a Jewess because she had converted to Islam and they should treat each other respectfully.

35 This *ḥadīth* is part of a long narration reported by Ibn ʿAbbās رَضِيَٱللَّهُعَنْهُمَا. It is found in al-Bukhārī, *Ṣaḥīḥ*, 2468, and Muslim, *Ṣaḥīḥ*, 1479. A short version reported by Umm Salama with wording similar to what al-Ghazālī has is also found in al-Bukhārī, *Ṣaḥīḥ*, 1910; Muslim, *Ṣaḥīḥ*, 1085.

256 ʿĀʾisha رَضِيَ ٱللَّهُ عَنْهَا reported that the Prophet صَلَّى ٱللَّهُ عَلَيْهِ وَسَلَّمَ said, "It is not permissible for a Muslim to abandon his brother for more than three days unless there is no safety against his misfortunes (*bawāʾiq*)."[36] This is made clear in specific cases. On this topic there is the statement of Ḥasan [b. ʿAlī] رَضِيَ ٱللَّهُ عَنْهُ who said, "Abandoning the fool is drawing near to God."[37] This certainly continues until death, for [we cannot] anticipate a cure for foolishness.

It was said to Muḥammad b. ʿUmar al-Wāqidī that a man abandoned another man until he died. He said, "This is something that has occurred with other people. Saʿd b. Abī Waqqāṣ abandoned ʿAmmār b. Yāsir until both died. ʿUthmān b. ʿAffān abandoned ʿAbd al-Raḥmān b. ʿAwf. ʿĀʾisha abandoned Ḥafṣa. Ṭāwūs abandoned Wahb b. Munabbih until he died."[38] All of this is premised on their opinion to safeguard themselves by abandoning [those people]. |

36 Ibn ʿAdī (d. 365/975 or 976), *al-Kāmil*, 6:146. Al-Khaṭṭābī reported it in *al-ʿUzla*, 47, and then said, "Muḥammad b. al-Ḥajjāj al-Muṣaffar [a sub-narrator] is not strong (*qawī*) according to the people of *ḥadīth*. However, the proofs of the Book, the *sunna*, and analogy, support the allowance of avoiding and separating from one from whose calamities there is no security. Moreover, it is obligatory on each person." Ed. note: This refers to leaving those who are troublemakers, or whose misfortunes are such that they will lead others into danger of disbelief.

37 Al-Khaṭṭābī, *al-ʿUzla*, 48; al-Daylamī, *Musnad al-firdaws*, 7004, from the *ḥadīth* of Ḥasan b. ʿAlī رَضِيَ ٱللَّهُ عَنْهُ.

38 Al-Khaṭṭābī, *al-ʿUzla*, 49. Al-Munāwī (d. 1031/1622) added other examples in *Fayḍ al-qadīr*, 6:234. He said, "al-Ḥasan [al-Baṣrī avoided] Ibn Sīrīn. Ibn al-Musayyab avoided his father, who was an olive oil merchant, and did not speak to him until he died. Al-Thawrī learned from Ibn Abī Laylā, and then avoided him. When Ibn Abī Laylā died, he did not attend his funeral. Ibn Ḥanbal avoided his uncle and his children because they accepted gifts of the sultan." Mālik, *al-Muwaṭṭaʾ*, 2:634, from ʿAṭāʾ b. Yasār that Muʿāwiya b. Abī Sufyān bought a gold or silver chalice for more than [the value of] its weight. Then Abū l-Dardāʾ said, "I heard the Messenger of God صَلَّى ٱللَّهُ عَلَيْهِ وَسَلَّمَ forbid that because it can only be like value for like value." Muʿāwiya said, "I do not see anything wrong with this." Then Abū l-Dardāʾ said, "Who will excuse me from Muʿāwiya? I informed him about the Messenger of God صَلَّى ٱللَّهُ عَلَيْهِ وَسَلَّمَ, and he informed me from his own opinion! I will not reside near you in any land where you reside." A note to the narration of al-Khaṭṭābī states, "The only reason Ṭāwūs avoided Wahb was because, at the end of his life, Wahb inclined toward the opinion of the Qadariyya [i.e., that there is absolute human free will] and proclaimed that to the people. Ṭāwūs blamed him for that. When he did not cease doing that, he became adverse to him and avoided him." Trans. note: The quote from al-Munāwī is in reference to the above mentioned *ḥadīth* "Whoever avoids his brother for a year is like the one who has shed his blood."

257 They present [another] argument based on a report about a man who went to a mountaintop to worship. He was brought to the Messenger of God صَلَّى ٱللَّهُ عَلَيْهِ وَسَلَّمَ, who said, "Neither you nor any among you should do that. If any one of you remains patient in some abode of Islam, then that is better for him than any one of you worshiping alone for forty years."[39]

It seems that this [narration came] at the beginning of Islam, in the context of [those who] abandoned fighting (*tark al-jihād*) when it was most needed. The evidence for this is the narration of Abū Hurayra رَضِيَ ٱللَّهُ عَنْهُ, who said,

> We went on a campaign during the time of the Messenger of God صَلَّى ٱللَّهُ عَلَيْهِ وَسَلَّمَ. We passed a canyon in which there was a stream with fresh water. One of the people said, "If only I could leave the people and stay in this canyon, but I will not do that until I mention it to the Messenger of God صَلَّى ٱللَّهُ عَلَيْهِ وَسَلَّمَ."
>
> Then [the Prophet] صَلَّى ٱللَّهُ عَلَيْهِ وَسَلَّمَ said, "Do not do it! The station of any one of you going out in the cause of God is better than his praying in his house for sixty years. Would you not like for God to forgive you and admit you into paradise? |
> 258 Campaign in the cause of God. If someone fights in the cause of God for even a brief time (*fuwāq nāqa*) God will admit him into paradise."[40]

They argue about what Muʿādh b. Jabal reported. He said that [the Messenger of God] صَلَّى ٱللَّهُ عَلَيْهِ وَسَلَّمَ said,

> Satan is a wolf among people, like a wolf among sheep. He comes from afar and from the side, and he comes for the stray one. So all of you beware of divisions (*shiʿāb*). It is incumbent on you to be with the people (*ʿāmma*), the congregation (*jamāʿa*), and [in] the mosques.[41]

---

39 Something similar was reported by al-Ṭayālisī (d. 204/819 or 820), *Musnad*, 1209; Abū Nuʿaym, *Maʿrifat al-ṣaḥāba*, 4:2260; and al-Bayhaqī, *Shuʿab al-īmān*, 9275. Trans. note: al-Zabīdī writes the chain of narrators is missing the Companion (*mursal*). Al-Zabīdī, *Itḥāf*, 6:337.

40 Al-Tirmidhī, *Sunan*, 1650, but he has seventy years instead of sixty. *Fuwāq nāqa* refers to the amount of time between two milkings of a she-camel.

41 Ibn Ḥanbal, *Musnad*, 5:232, 16:172, 16:200, and 16:200; and al-Ṭabarānī, *al-Muʿjam al-kabīr*, 20:164. Trans. note: al-Zabīdī said that the chain of narrators is missing

This narration refers to someone who wants to separate [himself] from others before [his acquisition of] knowledge is complete. We explain this below. [Separation] is prohibited except as a necessity. |

Mention of the Evidence of Those Inclined to Prefer Retreat 259

[These people] justify [retreat] with the statements of God تَعَالَىٰ about the story of Abraham عَلَيْهِ ٱلسَّلَامُ, *And I will leave you and those you invoke other than God and will invoke my Lord. I expect that I will not be in invocation to my Lord unhappy* [Q. 19:48]. Then God تَعَالَىٰ said, *So when he had left them and those they worshiped other than God, We gave him Isaac and Jacob, and each* [*of them*] *We made a prophet* [Q. 19:49]. [They argue that] this indicates that [Isaac and Jacob] were from the blessing of [Abraham's] retreat.

This is a weak [argument] because there is no benefit to socializing with disbelievers unless [one is] inviting them to the *dīn*. When there is hopelessness [because of] their [negative] response, then there is no recourse except to leave them; however, [there is a] statement about socializing with Muslims and the blessing in doing that was reported. When the Messenger of God صَلَّىٰ ٱللَّٰهُ عَلَيْهِ وَسَلَّمَ was asked, "What is more beloved to you, making ablutions from covered [private] vessels or from vessels from which people have already made ablutions?" He said, "From these used vessels, seek blessings from the hands of the Muslims."[42]

It was reported that when [the Messenger of God] صَلَّىٰ ٱللَّٰهُ عَلَيْهِ وَسَلَّمَ circumambulated the House [i.e., the Kaʿba], he went toward the well of Zamzam to drink from it. There were dates soaking in leather bags, and the people would press them with their hands and would eat from them | and drink. [The Prophet] came to drink and said, 260

---

one of the narrators (*munqaṭiʿ*). Al-Zabīdī, *Itḥāf*, 6:337.

42 Al-Ṭabarānī, *al-Muʿjam al-awsaṭ*, 798; Ibn ʿAdī, *al-Kāmil*, 2:374; and Abū Nuʿaym, *Ḥilya*, 8:203, from the *ḥadīth* narrated by Ibn ʿUmar رَضِيَ ٱللَّٰهُ عَنْهُمَا. The wording is, "Rather from these used vessels, for the *dīn* of God is pure and munificent." Then he said that the Messenger of God صَلَّىٰ ٱللَّٰهُ عَلَيْهِ وَسَلَّمَ used to request that water be brought in the used vessels. He would drink it, hoping for blessings from the hands of Muslims. This narration is also reported by ʿAbd al-Razzāq, *Muṣannaf*, 1:74, from Muḥammad b. Wāsiʿ but without the Companion from the chain of narrators (*mursal*).

> "Give me [something] to drink!"
>
> Al-ʿAbbās said, "This date juice (*nabīdh*) is a drink made by people putting their hands in it and mixing it. Do you not want me to bring you a cleaner drink than this, [a drink] from a sealed vessel in the House?"
>
> He said, "Give me this—I will drink from what the people drank from. I seek the blessing of the hands of the Muslims." Then he drank from it.[43]

So how can it be inferred from the [need] to separate from the disbelievers and [their] idols that [one should] separate from the Muslims, considering the increased blessings [of being] among them?

They also argue [using] the statement of Moses عَلَيْهِ ٱلسَّلَامُ, *But if you do not believe me, then leave me alone* [Q. 44:21]. He took refuge in retreat when despairing of them [i.e., Moses' people].

God تَعَالَىٰ said, concerning the companions of the cave, *And when you have withdrawn from them and that which they worship other than God, retreat to the cave. Your Lord will spread out for you of His mercy…* [Q. 18:16]. [God] ordered them to seclude themselves.

Our Prophet صَلَّى ٱللَّهُ عَلَيْهِ وَسَلَّمَ separated from the Quraysh when they harmed him and forced him to flee and enter the valley.[44] [The Prophet] also ordered his Companions to separate from [the Quraysh]
261 and migrate to Abyssinia.[45] | Then they joined him in Medina after God made His word supreme.

This separation is also [suitable] if [one] despairs of the disbelievers. He صَلَّى ٱللَّهُ عَلَيْهِ وَسَلَّمَ did not separate from Muslims, nor from any of the disbelievers whom he expected to accept Islam. The people of the

---

43 Reported by Ibn Ḥanbal, *Musnad*, 1:320, and al-Azraqī (d. 250/864), *Akhbār Makka*, 2:52–53, with similar wording. The basis of the narration is in al-Bukhārī, *Ṣaḥīḥ*, 1636. The wording used by al-Ghazālī is from Abū Ṭālib al-Makkī, *Qūt al-qulūb*, 2:234. Trans. note: The narration of al-Bukhārī does not mention date juice or include the statement "I seek the blessings from the hands of Muslims."

44 Ibn Saʿd, *Ṭabaqāt*, 1:177, with a connected chain of narrators (*mawṣūl*) and a chain missing the Companion (*mursal*). His report states that the polytheists were those who confined the tribe of Hāshim in the valley belonging to Abū Ṭālib. Al-Bayhaqī, *Dalāʾil*, 2:311, from the path of Mūsā b. ʿUqba al-Wāqidī, who is the author of *al-Maghāzī*. In this report, it states that Abū Ṭālib chose to enter it, and he was the one who ordered it.

45 Abū Dāwūd, *Sunan*, 3205.

cave did not separate from each other [because] they were believers. They only separated from the disbelievers. The consideration here is only about retreat from believers.

[Those who prefer retreat] also argue using the statement of [the Prophet] صَلَّىٱللَّهُعَلَيْهِوَسَلَّمَ to ʿAbdallāh b. ʿĀmir al-Juhanī who said, "O Messenger of God, what is salvation?" He said, "That your house suffices you, you restrain your tongue [so as to not harm] yourself, and you cry over your mistakes."[46]

It is reported that [the Prophet] صَلَّىٱللَّهُعَلَيْهِوَسَلَّمَ was asked,

> "Which person is most virtuous?"
>
> He said, "The believer, the one who struggles against himself and [with] his wealth in the cause of God تَعَالَىٰ."
>
> It was said, "Then who?"
>
> He said, "A man who separates [himself] in a valley to worship his Lord and spare people from his wickedness."[47]

He [the Prophet] صَلَّىٱللَّهُعَلَيْهِوَسَلَّمَ said, "God loves the servant who is pious, [financially] independent (*ghanī*), and unknown (*khafī*)."[48]

There are [points] to consider when using these *ḥadīth*s in an argument. With regard to [the Prophet's] صَلَّىٱللَّهُعَلَيْهِوَسَلَّمَ statement to ʿAbdallāh b. ʿĀmir, [the Prophet's] intuition (*tanzīlihi*) is only possible because he صَلَّىٱللَّهُعَلَيْهِوَسَلَّمَ knew of his [ʿAbdallāh b. ʿĀmir's] state | by way of the light of prophecy. Thus, the need to remain in 262
the house was most appropriate for [ʿAbdallāh b. ʿĀmir] and safer for him than socializing. So, he صَلَّىٱللَّهُعَلَيْهِوَسَلَّمَ did not order all the Companions to do that. Perhaps an individual maintains his safety by retreat rather than socializing, just as his safety lies in staying at home and not going out to fight (*jihād*). This does not prove that abandoning fighting is preferable.

---

46 Al-Tirmidhī, *Sunan*, 2406. Trans. note: The correct name according to al-Tirmidhī and others is ʿUqba b. ʿĀmir al-Juhanī. Al-Zabīdī, *Itḥāf*, 6:339.

47 Al-Bukhārī, *Ṣaḥīḥ*, 2786, and Muslim, *Ṣaḥīḥ*, 1888.

48 Muslim, *Ṣaḥīḥ*, 2965. Trans. note: The *ḥadīth* was transmitted by Saʿd b. Abī Waqqāṣ, who kept aloof from the conflicts of the Muslims after the death of the Prophet صَلَّىٱللَّهُعَلَيْهِوَسَلَّمَ. His son came to admonish him about this, and he mentioned this *ḥadīth*. Al-Zabīdī, *Itḥāf*, 6:339. Ed. note: Here "unknown" referes to the sense of one who does not draw attention to himself.

Socializing with people consists of striving and suffering (*mujāhada wa-muqāsā*). [About] this, he صَلَّى ٱللَّهُ عَلَيْهِ وَسَلَّمَ said, "The believer who socializes with people and is patient with their offenses is better than one who does not socialize with people and is not patient with their offenses."[49]

The statement of [the Prophet] صَلَّى ٱللَّهُ عَلَيْهِ وَسَلَّمَ mentioned above was revealed about "A man who separates [himself] in a valley to worship his Lord and spare the people his wickedness." This is a reference to one who is wicked by nature and harms people who socialize [with him].

And [the Prophet's] statement, "God loves [the servant] who is pious, [financially] independent (*ghanī*), and unknown (*khafī*)" indicates a preference for obscurity and guarding against fame, and this does not relate to retreat. How many monks (*rāhib*) are in retreat, but most people know about them? And how many [people] socialize with others but [live in] obscurity, no one mentions them and [they are] without fame? The reality of this matter is not related to retreat.

They argue about what was reported about a statement of [the Prophet] صَلَّى ٱللَّهُ عَلَيْهِ وَسَلَّمَ to his Companions,

> "Should I not inform you about the best of people?"
>
> They said, "Yes, O Messenger of God."
>
> Then he pointed with his hand to the west and said, "[He is] a man who [directs] the reins of his horse in the cause of God, anticipating that he will be victorious or be defeated. And should I not inform you of the best of people after him?"
>
> He pointed to the Hijaz and said, "A man who stays among
> 263 his sheep, | standing in prayer, paying the *zakāt*, and knowing
> the rights of God concerning his wealth. He withdrew from
> the wickedness of the people."[50]

49 Al-Tirmidhī, *Sunan*, 2507; Ibn Mājah, *Sunan*, 4032.

50 Mālik, *al-Muwaṭṭaʾ*, 2:45, with similar wording from ʿAṭāʾ b. Yasār but missing the Companion in the chain of narrators (*mursal*). It was also reported by Ibn Saʿd, *Ṭabaqāt*, 10:296, with the wording as given by al-Ghazālī, by al-Ṭabarānī, *al-Muʿjam al-kabīr*, 25:104, but with East instead of West, and by Ibn ʿAbd al-Barr (d. 463/1070 or 1071), *al-Tamhīd*, 17:450, but with greater Syria (Shām) instead of West.

So it is apparent that all these proofs do not reconcile the two opposing views. It is necessary to unveil its obscurity by clarifying the benefits of retreat and its dangers. A comparison of one with the other will explain the truth of the matter.

2

On the Benefits and the Corrupt Aspects of Retreat and Unveiling the Truth About Its Virtues

KNOW that people differ on this matter in the same way they differ about marriage and celibacy. We mentioned[1] that this matter varies according to the differences in individual states and personalities. This is in accordance with what we explained about the harms and benefits of marriage. The opinions here are similar.

We first mention the benefits of retreat, and divide them into religious (*dīniyya*) and worldly (*dunyāwiyya*) benefits.

The religious (*dīniyya*) [benefits] are divided into [two] abilities. One is the ability to learn obedience in seclusion through persistence in worship, contemplation (*fikr*), and instruction in knowledge. The [second] is freeing [oneself] from committing prohibited [acts] that people engage in through socializing, such as ostentatiousness (*riyāʾ*), backbiting, being silent [in the matter of] commanding good and forbidding evil, and inadvertently acquiring foul manners and filthy behavior from bad company.

The worldly [benefits] are also divided into the abilities one attains through seclusion, like the mastery of the professional [who focuses] on his seclusion. And [second], freeing [oneself] from the prohibitions that one is exposed to through socializing, like looking at the adornment of [this] world and the people seeking it, his covetousness for people and the peoples' covetousness for him, raising the veil of his generosity through socializing, being harmed

1 Book 12 of the *Revival of the Religious Sciences: The Proprieties of Marriage.*

by the wicked character of a companion, | or his suspicious thoughts, 265
slander, envy, or harm from his dimwittedness and vulgar character.

All of the benefits of retreat can be traced back to these [divisions]. So we arrange them [under] six benefits.

The first benefit is to completely focus on worship and contemplation. [This includes] becoming familiar with intimate [invocations to] God تَعَالَىٰ, instead of intimate conversation with people, and being occupied with unveiling the secrets of God تَعَالَىٰ concerning this world, the hereafter, and the dominion of the heavens and the earth.

Indeed, this requires focus without the distraction of socializing. Retreat is the means to attain [this first benefit]. And concerning this, a wise man said,

> No one is capable of seclusion except by clinging to the Book of God تَعَالَىٰ. Those who cling to the Book of God تَعَالَىٰ are those who retire from the world in remembrance of God. Those who remember God are with God, living in the remembrance of God, dying in the remembrance of God, and meeting God with the remembrance of God.

There is no doubt that socializing prohibits these people [i.e., who are distracted by socializing] from contemplation and remembrance; thus, retreat is best for them.

Similarly, during the beginning [of his prophecy], [the Prophet] صَلَّىٱللَّهُعَلَيْهِوَسَلَّمَ was alone at Mount Ḥirāʾ where he withdrew until he was strengthened by the light of prophecy.[2] Then [after the prophecy began] people no longer distracted him from God تَعَالَىٰ. In his heart he was near God while in his body he was with people to such an
extent that people | thought that Abū Bakr رَضِيَٱللَّهُعَنْهُ was his intimate 266
friend, but he صَلَّىٱللَّهُعَلَيْهِوَسَلَّمَ informed them about the depth of his focus on God when he said, "Were I to take an intimate friend, then I would take Abū Bakr as an intimate friend. But your companion [i.e., the Prophet] is the intimate friend of God."[3]

---

2 Al-Bukhārī, *Ṣaḥīḥ*, 4; Muslim, *Ṣaḥīḥ*, 160.

3 Al-Bukhārī, *Ṣaḥīḥ*, 466; Muslim, *Ṣaḥīḥ*, 2383. Al-Zabīdī writes, "The *ḥadīth* has numerous transmissions (*mutawātir*) and has been reported by as many as fifteen Companions." Al-Zabīdī, *Itḥāf*, 6:250.

The ability to combine socializing with people outwardly and drawing near God inwardly [comes from] the strength of prophethood.[4] So it is not appropriate for a weak person to deceive himself, and desire that [state].

It is likely that the rank of certain saints (*awliyāʾ*) reaches this point [of socializing with people while being near God]. It was reported that Junayd said, "I have been speaking with God for the past thirty years, but people think I am speaking to them."[5] This [state] is only made easy for one who is fully immersed in love for God, [who] leaves nothing for any other. This [state] should not be denied, for among the negligent who love created things, there might be one who socializes physically with people while not knowing what he says and what is said to him because of his excessive passion (*ʿishq*) for the object of his love. Moreover, there might be a person who is afflicted in his worldly affairs by a calamity that confuses him. Anxiety overwhelms him to such an extent that he socializes with people but does not perceive them and does not hear their voices, due to the severity of his distracted state. The matter of the hereafter is of greater [significance] according to intelligent [people], and there is
267 no | contradiction in this. However, what is of greatest importance for most people is seeking help through retreat, [to be immersed in love for God]. [About] this, it was said to a wise man, "What do they want by seclusion and by choosing retreat?" He said, "With this, they seek continual contemplation and the establishment of knowledge (*ʿulūm*) in their hearts, in order to live a delightful life and taste the sweetness of gnosis (*maʿrifa*)."[6]

---

4 Al-Zabīdī writes, "This means that prophethood directs itself to the world in the sense of conveying judgments [by way of revelation] to people and [prophethood directs itself] to the Truth (*al-ḥaqq*) in the sense of being present in front of Him and having familiarity through nearness. The first direction [i.e., conveying judgments to people] is the face of prophethood, and the second direction [i.e., toward the Truth] is the face of friendship (*wilāya*) [with God], which is the inner reality of prophethood (*sirr al-nubuwwa*) and its purity. Those who say that friendship is more virtuous than prophethood mean by this only the friendship of prophethood [i.e., being directed toward God, [a state] which can be achieved by pious saints, but they do not convey judgments to people]. The Prophet صَلَّى ٱللَّهُ عَلَيْهِ وَسَلَّمَ kept these two directions combined simultaneously." Al-Zabīdī, *Itḥāf*, 6:342.

5 Al-Kalābādhī (d. 380/990 or 991), *al-Taʿarruf li-madhhab ahl al-taṣawwuf*, 144.

6 Al-Dīnawarī (d. 333/944 or 945), *al-Majālisa wa-jawāhir al-ʿilm*, 43.

It was said to one of the monks (*ruhbān*), "What gives you the patience to remain alone?" He said, "I am not alone; I am a companion of God عَزَّوَجَلَّ. When I want Him to speak to me, I read His book. When I want to speak to Him, I pray."[7]

It was said to a wise man, "What benefit does asceticism and seclusion bring?" He said, "[it brings] intimacy with God."[8]

Sufyān b. ʿUyayna said,

> I met Ibrāhīm b. Adham رَحِمَهُ ٱللَّهُ in [greater] Syria (*bilād Shām*), and I said to him, "O Ibrāhīm, have you abandoned Khurāsān?"
>
> He said, "I only enjoy life here. I travel with my *dīn* from hilltop to hilltop, and whoever sees me says, 'he is bewitched, or a porter, or a salt merchant.'"[9] |

It was said to Ghazwān al-Raqāshī, "You are one of those who 268
do not laugh. What prevents you from sitting with your brothers?" He said, "I have found the comfort of my heart in the assembly of the one with whom I have need."[10]

It was said to Ḥasan [al-Baṣrī],

> "O Abū Saʿīd, there is a man whom we have never seen except when he is alone behind a pillar [of the mosque]."
>
> Ḥasan said, "When you see him, let me know."
>
> One day they saw him and said to Ḥasan, "That is the man we told you about." And they pointed to him.
>
> So Ḥasan went up to him and said, "O worshiper of God, I see that retreat is beloved to you. What prevents you from sitting with people?"
>
> He said, "There is a matter that distracts me from people."
>
> [Ḥasan] said, "And what prevents you from going to this man called Ḥasan and sitting with him?"

---

7 Trans. note: al-Zabīdī qualifies "fields of knowledge" by stating that it refers to *al-ʿulūm al-ilāhiyya* (theology). Al-Zabīdī, *Itḥāf*, 6:342.

8 Abū Nuʿaym, *Ḥilya*, 10:136.

9 Al-Dīnawarī, *al-Majālisa wa-jawāhir al-ʿilm*, 53; Abū Nuʿaym, *Ḥilya*, 7:369. The questioner in both narrations was Shaqīq b. Ibrāhīm, not Sufyān. The word *mawsūs* is an active participle (*fāʿil*), and means to speak to oneself. God تَعَالَىٰ says, ...*and [fully] know what his soul whispers to him* (*tuwaswisu bi-hi*)... (Q. 50:16).

10 Ibn Abī l-Dunyā, *al-ʿUzla wa-l-infirād*, 173.

> He said, "There is a matter that distracts me from people and from Ḥasan."
>
> Ḥasan said to him, "What is this distraction, may God have mercy on you?"
>
> He said, "From morning until evening I am caught between a blessing and a sin, so I think that I must preoccupy myself with thanking God for the blessing and seeking [His] forgiveness for the sin."
>
> Then Ḥasan said to him, "O worshiper of God, to me you are more knowledgeable than Ḥasan. So continue what you are doing."[11]

It was said that once Uways al-Qarnī was sitting while Harim b. Ḥayyān came to him. Uways said to him, "What brought you here?" He said, "I have come to get acquainted with you." Uways said, "I have never seen a person who truly knows his Lord seek to be acquainted with anyone else."[12] |

269 Al-Fuḍayl [b. ʿIyāḍ] said, "When I see the night coming, I rejoice and say, 'I can be alone with my Lord,' and when I see the morning overtaking me, I return to (*istarjiʿ*) the dislike of meeting people and those that come to me [who will] distract me from my Lord."[13]

ʿAbd al-Wāḥid b. Zayd said, "Give glad tidings to the one who lives in this world and lives in the hereafter." It was said to him, "How can that be?" He said, "He communicates with God in this world, and he is near Him in the hereafter."[14]

Dhū l-Nūn al-Miṣrī said, "The joy and delight of the believer is in seclusion while intimate communication with his Lord."[15]

---

11 Ibn Abī l-Dunyā, *al-ʿUzla wa-l-infirād*, 70.

12 Ibn Abī l-Dunyā, *al-ʿUzla wa-l-infirād*, 201. The narration reported by Harim from Uways states only that he said, "Remaining alone is beloved to me."

13 Abū Nuʿaym reported something similar to this from Sufyān al-Thawrī; Abū Nuʿāym, *Ḥilya*, 6:389. Trans. note: The verb *istarjaʿtu* also means to say *innā li-llāhi wa-innā ilayhi rājiʿūn* [we are from God and to Him we return].

14 Trans. note: Here the clarifications in brackets are from al-Zabīdī: "He communicates with God [through prayer] in this world, and he is near Him in the hereafter [as a reward for his prayer]." See al-Zabīdī, *Itḥāf*, 6:343.

15 Ibn Abī l-Dunyā, *al-ʿUzla wa-l-infirād*, 42, from "a worshiper in Yemen."

Mālik b. Dīnār said, "Whoever has not become accustomed to conversing with God عَزَّوَجَلَّ instead of conversing with people, then his knowledge is little, his heart is blind, and his life is wasted."[16]

Ibn al-Mubārak said, "How perfect is the state of whoever cuts off [all things to focus] on God تَعَالَىٰ."[17]

It was said that a righteous [man] said,

> While I was traveling in a particular region of [greater] Syria (*bilād al-Shām*), I met a worshiper who came out of [a cave] in one of the mountains. When he looked at me, he stepped aside toward the trunk of a tree and hid behind it.
>
> I said, "Glory be to God, you are being ungenerous toward me for [I am] looking at you."[18]
>
> Then he said, "O you! I have stayed in this mountain cave for a long time, healing my heart by abstaining from this world and its people. My labor in this has been long and my life has
> been spent in this. Then I asked God عَزَّوَجَلَّ | not to make my 270
> share of remaining days a struggle [in] my heart. Thus, God calmed [my heart] from confusion, [and made me] fond of solitude (*alf al-waḥda*) and isolation (*infirād*). But when I saw you, I feared that I would return to that earlier state. So leave me be! I seek refuge from your evil with the Lord of the gnostics and the Lover of the repentant."
>
> Then he shouted, "Oh! May He preserve me[19] from a long stay in this world."
>
> Then he turned his face from me and raised his hands, saying, "Leave me be, O world. Show your adornment to another, and deceive your people."
>
> Then he said, "Glory be to the One who causes the hearts of the gnostics to taste the delight of servitude and the sweetness of isolation for His sake, and oh how He diverts their hearts from thinking of gardens and beautiful maidens! And how He

---

16 Ibn Ḥibbān, *Rawḍat al-ʿuqalāʾ*, 85.

17 Al-Dīnawarī, *al-Majālisa wa-jawāhir al-ʿilm*, 592.

18 Ed. note: i.e., "You will not even let me see you?"

19 Ed. note: Here he speaks about himself in the third person.

> gathers their concerns for the remembrance of Him. For there is nothing sweeter to them than His intimate conversation."
>
> Then he left me and went away, saying, "Holy One! (*Quddūs*) Holy One (*Quddūs*)!"[20]

Thus it is in seclusion that there is familiarity with the remembrance of God and an increase in the gnosis (*maʿrifa*) of God. Similarly, in these [verses] it is said,[21]

> And I am surely veiled, and what for me is the veil
> perhaps an image of you has penetrated my mind.
>
> And I exit from the gathering, perhaps I
> speak of you alone concealed in my solitude.

[About] this, a wise man said,

> A person isolates himself to admonish his soul to free itself for moral excellence. At that point, he increases interaction
> 271 with people and releases himself from isolation | by being with them. Then when he is truly virtuous [with them], he seeks to be alone again to seek assistance in contemplation and to extract knowledge and wisdom.[22]

It was said, "Familiarity with people is one of the signs of impoverishment."[23]

So this [type of familiarity] is a great benefit, but it is [only] the reality for certain elites.

One [whose] constant remembrance becomes easy obtains a familiarity with God, or through constant reflection [he obtains] a realization of the knowledge of God. For him, solitude (*tajarrud*) is preferable to anything associated with socializing. The ultimate goal of worship and the fruit of mutual interaction (*muʿāmalāt*) is for a person to die as a lover of God, and as a knower (*ʿārif*) of God. There is no love except through an intimacy [with God] that

---

20 Abū Nuʿaym, *Ḥilya*, 9:356, with similar wording. Ed. note: *Quddūs* is one of the names of God.

21 These two verses are attributed to Majnūn Laylā (d. 68/687 or 688), *Dīwān*, 294, 296. They are also attributed to Qays b. Dharīḥ (d. 68/687 or 688), *Dīwān*, 161.

22 Al-Khaṭṭābī, *al-ʿUzla*, 23.

23 Al-Khaṭṭābī, *al-ʿUzla*, 23.

leads to constant remembrance. There is no gnosis (*maʿrifa*) except through constant reflection. An empty heart is a condition for each of these two [states], and there is no emptying [it] with socializing.

The second benefit: Retreat frees one from the disobedient [acts] that a person is exposed to primarily through socializing, and in seclusion he safeguards himself from them.

There are four [disobedient acts]: backbiting (*ghība*), ostentatiousness (*riyāʾ*), silence regarding commanding good and forbidding evil, and inadvertently acquiring vile manners and filthy behavior caused by eagerness for this world.

As for backbiting, if you are aware of the aspects of it mentioned in *Kitāb āfāt al-lisān*[24] in the Rubʿ al-Muhlikāt [Quarter of Perils],
| then you are aware that guarding oneself against [backbiting] 272
while socializing is a tremendous [challenge]. Only the veracious (*ṣiddīqūn*) can be saved from [backbiting]. The habit of most people is to constantly talk about the characteristics of other people, to joke about those [characteristics], and be amused by their pleasantries. This [type of talk] is their desire and delight. They seek comfort from their loneliness while in seclusion by turning to this [delight]. So if you socialize with them and agree with [their speech], then you have sinned and exposed yourself to the wrath of God تَعَالَىٰ. If you remain silent [as they talk], you are [their] partner, for the one who listens is also one of the backbiters. If you denounce them, they will hate you; they will abandon backbiting [the other person] and backbite you. Then they will increase [their] backbiting even more. Perhaps they will go beyond backbiting until they reach [the level of outright] contempt and vilification.

As for commanding good and forbidding evil, it is among the pillars of the *dīn* and an obligation, as will be explained at the end of this quarter [of the *Iḥyāʾ*].[25] If someone socializes with people, he cannot escape witnessing evil deeds. If he remains silent, he has disobeyed God; if he denounces [evil deeds], he is exposed to various types of harm. For example, seeking to free [someone] from one sin might drag him into disobedience greater than what

24 Book 24 of the *Revival of the Religious Sciences: The Bane of the Tongue.*

25 In Book 19 of the *Revival of the Religious Sciences: The Commanding of Right and the Forbidding of Wrong.*

was originally prohibited. In retreat is liberation from all this. So the neglect of [commanding good and forbidding evil] is a serious matter, and undertaking it is difficult.

Abū Bakr رَضِيَ ٱللَّهُ عَنْهُ stood to give a sermon and said, "O people, when you recite this verse, *O you who have believed, upon you is [responsibility for] yourselves. Those who have gone astray will not harm you when you have been guided...* [Q. 5:105], you are applying it in the wrong way. I have heard the Messenger of God صَلَّى ٱللَّهُ عَلَيْهِ وَسَلَّمَ
273 say, 'When the people see an evil act, but do not | change it, then soon God will send punishment to them all.'"[26]

[The Prophet] صَلَّى ٱللَّهُ عَلَيْهِ وَسَلَّمَ said, "God will [continue] asking His servant until He says, 'What prevented you, when you saw an evil act in this world, from denouncing it?' When God allows His servant to present his evidence, he will say, 'O my Lord, I had hope in You and fear of the people.'"[27]

This is [the case] when one fears being hit [when denouncing evil] or [facing] an unbearable matter. Knowing the limits of this is difficult, and there is danger in it. Thus retreat offers an escape [from it]. Also, commanding good and forbidding evil causes disputes and foments internal havoc in [people's] hearts. [A verse of poetry] states,

> And how often have I brought in the wake of your actions good advice;
> and all that is gained is anger for the one giving advice.[28]

---

26 Abū Dāwūd, *Sunan*, 4338; al-Tirmidhī, *Sunan*, 2168; al-Nasāʾī, *al-Sunan al-kubrā*, 11092; and Ibn Mājah, *Sunan*, 4005.

27 Ibn Mājah, *Sunan*, 4017, but with the statement "I was frightened (*fariqtu*) of the people." The wording given by al-Ghazālī was reported by al-Khaṭṭābī, *al-ʿUzla*, 67. After the narration, he said, "This path of transmission is preferred by the transmitters among the scholars of *ḥadīth*. Based on this, a man does not commit a sin, God willing, if he abandons confronting people of evil acts when he fears their enmity and is not safe from their evil aggression. This is [true] as long as he hates their acts in his heart and cuts himself off from them through his determination and intention." Then al-Khaṭṭābī presented various statements on the benefit of retreat specific to this topic.

28 Al-Khaṭṭābī reported this verse of poetry in *al-ʿUzla*, 38; see also al-Mubarrad (d. 285/998), *al-Kāmil*, 3:1502, from al-Riyāshī; and ʿUmāra b. ʿAqīl (d. 239/853 or 854), *Dīwān*, 92.

Whoever has experience in commanding good has often regretted it. It is similar to the person who wants to straighten a leaning wall that is about to fall on him; when it falls on him, he says, "O if only I had left it leaning!" |

Indeed, if he had found some assistants to hold up the wall so 274
he could stabilize it with a pillar, then he [could have] straightened it. Today you will not find assistants, so leave [the evildoers] and save yourself.

As for ostentation, it is a distressing disease that is difficult [even] for the substitutes (*abdāl*) and the pillars (*awtād*)[29] to guard against. Whoever socializes with people must persuade them; whoever persuades them must show off;[30] whoever [is] ostentatious [toward people] falls into what they have fallen into and is destroyed just as they were destroyed.

The least of what relates to [ostentation] is hypocrisy (*nifāq*). If you intervene between two enemies and do not agree with either one of them, you will be hated by both of them simultaneously. If you insincerely advise both of them, you will become one of the most evil people.[31] As [the Prophet] ﷺ said, "You will find among the most evil people [those that] are two-faced, [he] who comes to some with one face and to others with [another] face."[32]

The least of what is necessary for socializing with people is to display a desire [to be with them] and exaggerate it. There is no escaping [the fact] that this involves lying, either at its core or in its excess. Then there is the display of compassion by asking about [his] condition by saying to him, "How are you?" and "How is your family?" While in your heart, you have no real concern about his problems. [This is] pure hypocrisy. Ibn Masʿūd said,

> A man among you leaves his house, and another man in need
> meets him and says such and such. | [The first man] then 275

29 Trans. note: The "substitutes" (*abdāl*) and the "pillars" (*awtād*) are levels in the Sufi hierarchy of saints. See Schimmel, *Mystical Dimensions of Islam*, 200–202.

30 Trans. note: al-Zabīdī states that these last two sentences were mentioned in Abū Ṭālib al-Makkī, *Qūt al-qulūb*, traced back to Sufyān al-Thawrī, and in al-Qushayrī, *al-Risāla*, traced back to Yaḥyā b. Abī Kathīr. Al-Zabīdī, *Itḥāf*, 6:347.

31 The exception to this is when the intention is to bring about reconciliation. Al-Zabīdī, *Itḥāf*, 6:346.

32 Al-Bukhārī, *Ṣaḥīḥ*, 3494; Muslim, *Ṣaḥīḥ*, 2526.

> responds by praising [the other man] while not mentioning anything about his need. Then [the first man] returns home and God is angry with him for he has nothing of his *dīn*.[33]

Sarī [al-Saqaṭī] said, "If my brother were to come to me, I would straighten my beard with my hand when he enters, but be fearful that [my action] would be written in the register of the hypocrites."[34]

Al-Fuḍayl [b. ʿIyāḍ] was sitting alone in the sacred mosque [in Mecca, near the Kaʿba] and his [Muslim] brother came to him, and [al-Fuḍayl] said to him,

> "What brings you here?"
>
> He said, "Friendliness, O Abū ʿAlī."
>
> He said, "By God, that is similar to being alone. Is it that you want to make me look good and that I make you look good? You will lie to me, and I will lie to you. Then either you will get up and leave me, or I will get up and leave you."[35]

One of the scholars said, "God does not love a servant except that He loves for him not to have fame."[36]

Ṭāwūs [b. Kaysān] entered [the room of] the [Umayyad] caliph Hishām [b. ʿAbd al-Malik] and said, "How are you, O Hishām?" He became angry and said, "Why do you not address me as the Commander of the Believers?" [Ṭāwūs] said, "That is because most of the Muslims do not agree on your caliphate, and I fear that I would be a liar."

Thus, one who is capable of guarding himself [from ostentation] can socialize with people. If not, then he should be content to have his name confirmed in the register of hypocrites. The predecessors (*salaf*) would meet each other and be cautious of their questions, [such as] "How are you this morning?" or "How are you this evening?"
276 or "How are you?" or "How are you feeling?" | and their responses.

33 Al-Faryābī (d. 301/913 or 914), *Ṣifat al-nifāq*, 87. Ed. note: The first man should have stated his need and allowed his Muslim brother to help him.

34 Ed. note: This refers to Sarī l-Saqaṭī's sensitivity—he was concerned that he might be considered a hypocrite for the small act of straightening his beard to seem more presentable to his Muslim brother, and that this might be seen as ostentatiousness, or doing something that is not for the sake of God.

35 Ibn Abī l-Dunyā, *al-ʿUzla wa-l-infirād*, 72.

36 Al-Dīnawarī, *al-Majālisa wa-jawāhir al-ʿilm*, 166.

They used to ask each other about the condition of the *dīn*, not about the condition of this world.[37]

Ḥātim al-Aṣamm said to Ḥāmid al-Laffāf, "How are you, in your soul?" He said, "Safe and pardoned." Ḥātim disliked his answer and said, "O Ḥāmid, safety comes after the *ṣirāṭ* and pardon comes in heaven."[38]

When it was said to Jesus عَلَيْهِ ٱلسَّلَامُ, "How is your morning?" he would say, "I arose with no power over the benefit I seek and unable to fend off what I guard against. I arose in debt [due to] my actions, and all good is in the hand of another [i.e., God]. So there is no one more in need than I."[39]

When anyone said to al-Rabīʿ b. Khuthaym "How is your morning?" he said, "We arose in the morning as weak sinners. We receive our provisions, and we await our appointed times."[40]

When anyone said to Abū l-Dardāʾ "How is your morning?" he said, "I arose with goodness if I have been saved from the fire."

When anyone said to Sufyān al-Thawrī "How is your morning?" he said, "I arose complaining about this and that, blaming this and that, and fleeing from this and that."

It was said to Uways al-Qarnī, "How is your morning?" He said, "How is a man who last evening did not know if he would wake up, and he arose this morning not knowing if he will [live] to the evening?" |

It was said to Mālik b. Dīnār, "How is your morning?" He said, 277
"I arose with a lifespan diminishing and sins increasing."

It was said to a wise man, "How is your morning?" He said, "I arose displeased with my life [as it proceeds] to my death, and [displeased] with my soul [as it proceeds] to my Lord."

It was said to a wise man, "How is your morning?" He said, "I arose eating the provisions of my Lord while obeying His enemy Iblīs."

---

37 Abū Ṭālib al-Makkī, *Qūt al-qulūb*, 1:163.

38 The *ṣirāṭ* refers to the bridge over hell that all souls must cross. All those who safely cross the bridge will go to paradise.

39 Ibn Abī Shayba (d. 235/849 or 850), *al-Muṣannaf*, 29999, 35377.

40 Ibn al-Mubārak, *al-Zuhd*, 151, in the addendum of narrations from Nuʿaym b. Ḥammād.

It was said to Muḥammad b. Wāsiʿ, "How is your morning?" He said, "What do you think of a man who is traveling every day to the hereafter, in stages?"[41]

It was said to Ḥāmid al-Laffāf, "How is your morning?" He said, "I arose desiring health from day to night." He was asked, "Are you not healthy every day?" He said, "Health [to me, means] a day when I do not disobey God تعالى."[42]

It was said to a man with a fatal illness, "What is your condition?" He said, "What is the condition of someone who intends to embark on a long journey with no provisions, who will enter a grave all alone without a companion, and who will go before a just king but without any evidence [in his favor]?"[43] |

278 It was said to Ḥassān b. Abī Sinān, "What is your condition?" He said, "What is the condition of someone who will die, then be raised, and then be held accountable."[44]

Ibn Sīrīn said to a man,

> "What is your condition?"
>
> He said, "What is the condition of a man who owes five hundred dirhams and has a family to care for?"
>
> Ibn Sīrīn entered his house and emerged with one thousand dirhams. He gave it to [the man] and said, "Five hundred [dirhams] are to pay off your debt, and five hundred [dirhams] are for you and your family."
>
> That was all that he had, so he said, "By God, I will never ask anyone about his condition again."

[Ibn Sīrīn] did that only because he feared that asking without any [real] concern for the other's affair would make him an ostentatious hypocrite. [The predecessors] asked about the affairs of the *dīn* and the states of the hearts [of those] in the service of God (*fī muʿāmalat Allāh*). If they asked about the affairs of this world, it

41 Abū Nuʿaym, *Ḥilya*, 2:348; and Ibn ʿAsākir (d. 571/1175 or 1176), *Tārīkh madīnat Dimashq*, 56:169.

42 Al-Bayhaqī, *Shuʿab al-īmān*, 6858; al-Qushayrī, *al-Risāla*, from Ḥāmid al-Laffāf from his shaykh Ḥātim al-Aṣamm.

43 Transmitted by Ibn Qutayba (d. 276/889 or 890), *ʿUyūn al-akhbār*, 2:31, from a wise man of Persia.

44 Al-Bayhaqī, *al-Zuhd al-kabīr*, 565.

would have been out of a [real] concern and a determination to correct any need that presented itself.

One of them said,

> I know people who would not meet each other (*yatalāqawn*)[45] except that were any of them to make a request for all that his companion possessed, [the companion] would not deny him. However, today I see people who meet each other and [even] ask about the condition of a chicken in the house, and were any of them to presume even to request a seed of his companion's wealth, he would deny him. So is this not all merely ostentation and hypocrisy?[46]

As a sign of this, you will see [someone] say, "How are you?" Then the other will say, "How | are you?" Each questioner does 279
not expect a response, each one is busy asking the question and gives no response. This [occurs] because they both know that it is for ostentation and affectation. Perhaps it is because [their] hearts possess rancor and malice [while their] tongues utter the question.

Ḥasan [al-Baṣrī] said,

> By God, when hearts were secure they used to say, "Peace be upon you." However, today [they say], "How are you this morning, may God pardon you?" or "How are you, may God make you sound?" If we accept their statement, then it is an innovation (*bidᶜa*). No, we will not accept this. If they desire, let them become angry with us, and if they desire, let them not [be angry].[47]

He said this because starting your statement with "How are you this morning?" is an innovation.[48]

A man said to Abū Bakr b. Ayyāsh,

> "How are you this morning?"

45 Edition B states "they flatter each other" (*yatamāliqūn*), and the other term is copied in the margin.

46 Trans. note: al-Zabīdī states that this narration is in Abū Ṭālib al-Makkī, *Qūt al-qulūb*. See al-Zabīdī, *Itḥāf*, 6:349.

47 Abū Ṭālib al-Makkī, *Qūt al-qulūb*, 1:163.

48 A narration states, "If someone begins speaking to you before greeting you with peace, then do not respond to him." Al-Zabīdī, *Itḥāf*, 6:349.

> He did not answer him but [instead] said, "They invite us to this innovation."
>
> He [also] said, "This [way of greeting] first started during the time of the plague, [referring to] the plague of Emmaus in Syria, which brought rapid death. A man would meet his friend in the morning and say, "How are you this morning as to the plague?" When he would meet him in the evening, he would say, "How are you this evening?"[49] |

280 [This] means that meetings in most common situations are not without various types of mannerisms, ostentation, and hypocrisy; all of that is blameworthy. Some of it is prohibited (*maḥẓūr*), and some of it is disliked (*makrūh*). Retreat is an escape from that. If someone meets people and does not treat them according to their customs, they will hate him, consider him annoying, backbite [about] him, and prepare to harm him. They lose their *dīn* that way, and he loses his *dīn* and worldly life by taking revenge against them.

As for acquiring the disposition of the manners and actions of the people one observes, this is a hidden disease. Intelligent people rarely notice this, much less the heedless. A person should not sit with a corrupt person for a long time, while he rejects him internally. The exception would be if he takes measure of himself before sitting [with the corrupt person], so that he realizes the difference [between them] and [reaffirms] his dislike of corruption and its onerousness. Continually observing corruption allows it to ease its way into [one's] disposition; then his [negative] impression of [the corruption] and understanding of its severity falls away. It is only the one who restrains himself from [corruption] who [ultimately senses] the severity of its occurrence in the heart. So, if long observance of it makes it insignificant then it is nearly impossible to have the strength to restrain [oneself], and [one's] disposition quickly humbles itself and inclines toward [corruption] or something close to it. Perhaps the extended observance of someone else's major [sins] makes

---

49 Abū Ṭālib al-Makkī, *Qūt al-qulūb*, 1:163. The plague of Emmaus was the first plague to appear in the Islamic period (in 639 CE during the caliphate of ʿUmar). It is associated with Emmaus, which is six miles from Jerusalem. It is said that the name [Ar. ʿAmwās] was derived from *ʿamm* (tribe) and *āsā* (mourns), making it a compound word. Al-Zabīdī, *Itḥāf*, 6:350.

one's own minor [sins] seem paltry. So one who is always looking at the wealthy finds fault with the bounties that God has given him. Sitting with [the wealthy] causes one to belittle what he has, while sitting among the poor causes one to magnify the bounties that have been given to him.

So observing obedient people and disobedient people has an effect on [one's] disposition. Whoever limits his view to the conditions of the Companions and the Followers [with regard] to [their] worship
and [state] far above this world | will continue to view himself as 281
insignificant, and his worship as paltry. As long as he sees himself as deficient, then he will have the motivation to strive, desiring perfection and completion by imitating [them].

Whoever looks at the conditions of most people at this time—at their rejection of God تَعَالَىٰ, their acceptance of this world, and their frequent disobedience—would then magnify in himself even the smallest desire for good he comes across in his heart, and this [marks the state of his heart's] destruction.

Just hearing about good and evil is enough to alter a disposition, even without witnessing it. Regarding this detail, one can know the inner meaning of this statement of [the Prophet] صَلَّىٱللَّهُ عَلَيْهِ وَسَلَّمَ, "At the mention of the righteous people, mercy descends."[50] The only mercy to be desired is entry into heaven and the meeting with God تَعَالَىٰ. [Mercy] itself does not descend at the mention of [the righteous], rather [mentioning them] is a cause of attaining it. [Mercy] is the rousing of desire in the heart and eagerness to imitate [the righteous]. It also disdains any deficiency or shortcoming that would obscure it. The origin of mercy is doing good; the origin of doing good is the desire; the origin of the desire is remembering the states of the righteous. This is the meaning of the descent of mercy [in this *ḥadīth*].[51]

---

50 Abū Nuʿaym, *Ḥilya*, 7:285, as the statement of Sufyān b. ʿUyayna. It is not attributed to the Prophet صَلَّىٱللَّهُ عَلَيْهِ وَسَلَّمَ. See also Ibn al-Ṣalāḥ, *Muqaddima Ibn al-Ṣalāḥ*, 428. See al-Zabīdī, *Itḥāf*, 6:351.

51 Trans. note: al-Zabīdī clarifies that mentioning the righteous is generally accompanied by the mention of God, and this is what brings down mercy. The righteous person seeks forgiveness from God for his sins and seeks His acceptance of his good deeds. Also, at the gathering of the righteous, angels descend and cover them with mercy. Al-Zabīdī, *Itḥāf*, 6:351.

What intelligent people understand from the intended meaning of this statement is also understood from its opposite. At the mention of corrupt people, a curse descends because mentioning them often makes it easier for [one's] disposition to accept disobedience. A curse is distance [from God]; the origin of distance from God is
282 disobedience and turning away | from God by welcoming worldly pleasure and immediate desires that do not accord with the law. The origin of disobedience [is seeing it] as insignificant [lit., weightless] and [no longer] an abomination from the heart. The origin of the insignificance [of these acts in the heart] is familiarity with their occurrence by frequently hearing about them.

And if this is the situation [when just] talking about the righteous and the corrupt [people], what do you think [if you] witness them. Indeed, the Messenger of God صَلَّى ٱللَّٰهُ عَلَيْهِ وَسَلَّمَ clarified this when he said, "The example of the gathering of evil is the example of the [blacksmith's] bellow. The harm from it will either burn you or its smell will affect you." That is, the odor will be on one's clothes even if [one] does not feel it. Likewise, corruption eases its way into the heart, and one is not aware of it. Then he صَلَّى ٱللَّٰهُ عَلَيْهِ وَسَلَّمَ said, "The example of the gathering of the righteous is the example of the perfume seller. Even if he does not give you any, you experience his aroma."[52]

[About] this, I say that if someone notices a lapse from a scholar, he is forbidden to talk about it. There are two reasons for this. The first reason is that it is backbiting.

The second reason is the greater of the two. Talking about the lapse minimizes it for the people who hear about it. Their concern for the significance of daring to [commit a similar lapse] then slips from their hearts. This [becomes] a cause that facilitates this disobedience. Perhaps someone [who] dares to do this then feels disdain for it, and he might push away the disdain by saying, "How could we avoid this while we are all compelled to similar things, even the scholars and worshipers." |

283 If he thinks that a scholar would not dare do such an act [a lapse], and not [even] give it a passing thought, he would be fearful

52 Both of these quotes are reported as one *ḥadīth* in al-Bukhārī, *Ṣaḥīḥ*, 2101; Muslim, *Ṣaḥīḥ*, 2628. This version of the *ḥadīth* is reported by Ibn Ḥibbān, *Ṣaḥīḥ*, 579.

of daring to do it [i.e., committing an act of disobedience]. How many people rush after this world and are eager to acquire it? Such a person destroys himself over the love of leadership and its adornments. He deems the foulness of [love for leadership] to be insignificant, and he insists that the Companions رَضِيَ ٱللَّهُ عَنْهُمْ did not hold themselves back from the love of leadership. He might even give as evidence the fighting between ʿAlī and Muʿāwiya رَضِيَ ٱللَّهُ عَنْهُمَا.[53] He speculates to himself that it [i.e., the fighting] was not in pursuit of the truth but rather in pursuit of leadership. This mistaken belief minimizes for him the matter of leadership and the [acts of] disobedience connected to [leadership].

One with an ignoble disposition tends to follow errors and turn away from good [deeds]. In fact, [his] calculation of [what is an] error is based on his desire at that moment and [he uses it] as a justification. This is among the detailed plans of Satan. In the following verse God describes those who forsake Satan concerning these things [as those] *Who listen to speech and follow the best of it…* [Q. 39:18].

[The Prophet] صَلَّى ٱللَّهُ عَلَيْهِ وَسَلَّمَ gave a parable for this when he said,

> The example of a person who sits and listens to wisdom but then acts only according to any evil he hears is like the example of a man who goes to a shepherd and says, "O shepherd, give me one of your sheep to slaughter."
>
> [The shepherd] says, "Go and choose the best of them."
>
> So he goes and grabs the ear of the sheepdog.[54]

Whoever reports the lapses of the leaders (*aʾimma*) is just like this.

Another indication that the repeated occurrence and constant witnessing of a thing causes [the seriousness of it] to fall from
the heart is [clear from] the manner in which most people | react 284
when they see a Muslim eating during the day in Ramaḍān. They ostracize him, nearly reaching the point that they consider him to be a disbeliever. They might know someone who postpones the [obligatory] prayers beyond their times. Yet their dispositions

53 Trans. note: This refers to the battle of Ṣiffīn in the year 37/657. Al-Zabīdī, *Itḥāf*, 6:352.

54 Ibn Mājah, *Sunan*, 4172.

keep them from fleeing from him as they flee from [one who] puts off the fast, even though the [intentional] abandonment of one prayer is determined to be disbelief according to most people and [deserving of] capital punishment, and abandoning the fast in Ramaḍān, even all of it, is not determined [to be disbelief]. There is no reason for [these differences] except that prayer is repeated; it is taken lightly because of its frequency, so its impact falls, with experience, from the heart.

Likewise, were a legal scholar (*faqīh*) to wear a silk garment, or a gold ring, or drink from a silver vessel, people would distance themselves [from him], and severely denounce him. Yet in a long assembly [with him] they might observe that he does not speak without backbiting people. Yet they do not distance themselves from him for that, and backbiting is worse than adultery (*zinā*).[55] Then how is [this] not worse than wearing a silk garment? [Because we] often hear and witness backbiting, its impact [diminishes in our] hearts, and [backbiting becomes] an easy matter for people.

So make sure you understand these details and flee from people as if you were fleeing from a lion. You will not witness anything from them, except that it will increase your eagerness for this world and your negligence of the hereafter. It will make disobedience easy |
285 for you and weaken your yearning for obedience.

If you find someone whose manner and comportment remind you of God, then stick to him and do not leave him. Seize hold of him and do not demean him, for he is the treasure of the rational man and the lost [treasure] of the believer. Realize that a righteous companion is better than solitude, and solitude is better than an evil companion. When you have understood these concepts, and considered your disposition, and paid close attention to the state of the one you want to socialize with, then it should be apparent to

---

55 There is a *ḥadīth* reported by Hannād (d. 243/857 or 858), *al-Zuhd*, 1178; al-Ṭabarānī, *al-Muʿjam al-awsaṭ*, 6586; and al-Bayhaqī, *Shuʿab al-īmān*, 6315, 6316, as attributed to the Prophet صَلَّى ٱللَّٰهُ عَلَيْهِ وَسَلَّمَ: "Beware of backbiting, for backbiting is more severe than fornication or adultery (*zinā*)." They said, "O Messenger of God, how can backbiting be more severe than *zinā*?" He said, "If a man commits *zinā* and then repents, God will accept his repentance. But God will not forgive the one who backbites [someone] until the one whom he backbites forgives him."

you whether the more suitable [action] is distancing [oneself] from him in retreat or drawing near by socializing with him.

Take care that you do not make absolute judgments in favor of retreat or socializing because for every clear distinction requiring an absolute statement, either no or yes, there is a clear consequence. It is not a true distinction unless it has a distinguishing marker.

The third benefit [of retreat]: Freedom from tribulations and controversies. It also guards the *dīn* and soul and protects a person from falling into [tribulations and controversies] and being exposed to their dangers.

Rarely is a city free from difficulties, tribulations, and controversies. So withdrawing from [people leads to] safety. ʿAbdallāh b. ʿAmr b. al-ʿĀṣ said that when the Messenger of God صَلَّى ٱللَّهُ عَلَيْهِ وَسَلَّمَ mentioned the tribulations, he described them by saying,

> "You see people breaking their covenants, belittling their trusts, and becoming like this." Then he intertwined his fingers.
>
> So I said, "What do you order me to do?"
>
> He said, "Stay in your house, control your tongue, take from what you know, | and leave what you reject. Take care of your 286
> own affair, and abandon the affair of other people."[56]

Abū Saʿīd al-Khudrī reported that [the Prophet] صَلَّى ٱللَّهُ عَلَيْهِ وَسَلَّمَ said, "There will soon be a time when the best wealth of a Muslim will be sheep that he takes to the tops of the mountains [where there are] areas of rainfall, fleeing with his *dīn* from tribulations, going from mountaintop to mountaintop."[57]

ʿAbdallāh b. Masʿūd reported that [the Prophet] صَلَّى ٱللَّهُ عَلَيْهِ وَسَلَّمَ said,

---

56 Abū Dāwūd, *Sunan*, 4343; al-Nasāʾī, *al-Sunan al-kubrā*, 9962. Al-Khaṭṭābī said in *al-ʿUzla*, 15, when commenting on this narration, "Your own affair (*amr al-khāṣṣa*) refers to all that is specific to a person and concerns him. Each person should focus on himself and on the care of his family and possessions. He should maintain them and strive to make their affair sound. He صَلَّى ٱللَّهُ عَلَيْهِ وَسَلَّمَ forbade him from dealing with the affairs of the common people and becoming involved in governing them, leading them, and mediating in their affairs. Thus, he صَلَّى ٱللَّهُ عَلَيْهِ وَسَلَّمَ said, '…abandoning the affair of other people.'" This is the context that al-Ghazālī used.

57 Al-Bukhārī, *Ṣaḥīḥ*, 19. Trans. note: The *ḥadīth* in al-Bukhārī does not have the final statement "going from mountaintop to mountaintop."

> "A time will come when there is no safety for one who has *dīn*, unless he flees with his *dīn* from town to town, and from mountaintop to mountaintop, and cave to cave, like a fox on the prowl."
>
> It was said to him, "When will that be, O Messenger of God?"
>
> He said, "When one's livelihood cannot be attained without disobedience to God تَعَالَىٰ. When that time comes, celibacy is allowable."
>
> They said, "How is that possible, O Messenger of God, when you have ordered us to marry?"
>
> He said, "When that time comes, the destruction of a man will be at the hands of his parents. If he has no parents [living], it will be at the hands of his wife and children. If he has no [family], then at the hands of his relatives."
>
> They said, "How will that be, O Messenger of God?"
>
> 287 He said, | "They will criticize him for being tightfisted. Then he will undertake [affairs] for which he is not suited until they drive him to [sources of] destruction."[58]

Even though this narration refers to celibacy, it is understood that it includes retreat because the one who maintains a family is not free from earning a livelihood and socializing. Thus, he cannot attain a livelihood without disobedience to God تَعَالَىٰ.

I am not saying that now is the time [referred to in the narration]. It was [many] periods before this time.[59] And [about] that [period], Sufyān al-Thawrī said, "By God, retreat is allowable."[60]

Ibn Masʿūd رَضِيَ ٱللَّهُ عَنْهُ said,

> The Messenger of God صَلَّى ٱللَّهُ عَلَيْهِ وَسَلَّمَ mentioned the tribulation and the days of *al-harj*. I asked him, "What is *al-harj*?"
>
> He said, "It is a time when a man is not safe from the one sitting next to him."
>
> I said, "What do you order me to do if I reach that time?"

58 Al-Bayhaqī, *al-Zuhd al-kabīr*, 439; al-Daylamī (d. 509/1115 or 1116), *Musnad al-firdaws*, no. 8697. The wording here is from al-Khaṭṭābī, *al-ʿUzla*, 9.

59 Ed. note: This refers to al-Ghazālī's time.

60 Abū Nuʿaym, *Ḥilya*, 6:388.

> He said, "Restrain yourself and your hand and stay in your house."
>
> I said, "O Messenger of God, what is your opinion, if someone should enter my house?"
>
> He said, "Lock yourself in your house."
>
> I said, "And if he enters my house?"
>
> He said, "Then go to your place of prayer [in your house] and do this—and he grabbed his wrist—and say, 'My Lord is God' (*rabbī Allāh*) until you die."[61]

When he was called to [go on] campaign during the time of Muʿāwiya, Saʿd [b. Abī Waqqāṣ][62] said,

> "No, unless you give me a sword that has two good eyes and a tongue that announces this one is a disbeliever, so I can kill him, and [this one is] a believer, so I can hold off [from killing him]."
>
> He [continued and] said, "Our likeness and your likeness is the example of a people who were on a clear path."
>
> Thus, [the people] traveled | in such a state. Then a violent wind 288
> stirred, and they lost the way, as it became unclear to them.
>
> Some of them said, "The path is to the right."
>
> So they took it but became confused and went astray.
>
> Some of them said, "The path is to the left." So they took it but became confused and went astray. The rest of them sat and waited until the wind had ceased and the path became clear.
>
> So Saʿd and a group withdrew from the tribulations (*fitan*) and did not interact with anyone until after the tribulations ended.[63]

61 Abū Dāwūd, *Sunan*, 4258, in abbreviated form. The full narration is reported in al-Khaṭṭābī, *al-ʿUzla*, 11.

62 Trans. note: al-Zabīdī reported that this occurred during the first civil war after the death of the third caliph ʿUthmān. Saʿd was approached by both his son, ʿUmar, and his nephew, Hāshim b. ʿUtba. ʿUmar was trying to recruit him on behalf of Muʿāwiya, and Hāshim on behalf of ʿAlī. Al-Zabīdī, *Itḥāf*, 6:355.

63 Al-Khaṭṭābī, *al-ʿUzla*, 17.

It was reported from Ibn ʿUmar رَضِيَ ٱللَّهُ عَنْهُمَا that when news reached him that Ḥusayn [b. ʿAlī] رَضِيَ ٱللَّهُ عَنْهُمَا [left Medina] heading toward Iraq, he followed him, and traveled with him for three days.

> [Ibn ʿUmar رَضِيَ ٱللَّهُ عَنْهُمَا] said to [Ḥusayn رَضِيَ ٱللَّهُ عَنْهُمَا] "Where are you going?"
>
> He said, "Iraq."
>
> Ḥusayn brought many books and tomes (*ṭawāmīr*)[64] with him, and [Ḥusayn] said, "These are their books and their pledges of allegiance."
>
> [Ibn ʿUmar] said, "Pay no attention to their books and do not go to them."[65]
>
> [Ḥusayn] refused [i.e., he went to them].
>
> So [Ibn ʿUmar] said to [Ḥusayn], "I am going to narrate a *ḥadīth* to you. Gabriel came to the Prophet صَلَّى ٱللَّهُ عَلَيْهِ وَسَلَّمَ and gave him a choice between this world and the hereafter. [The Prophet] chose the hereafter over this world. You are a part of the [family of the] Messenger of God صَلَّى ٱللَّهُ عَلَيْهِ وَسَلَّمَ, and by God, not one of you will ever rule [as caliph]. Nothing is diverting you from [the caliphate] except that which is better for you."
>
> [Ḥusayn] refused to return [to Medina]. Ibn ʿUmar embraced him and began to cry, saying, "I entrust you to God [to safeguard you] from death or captivity."[66] |

289 The Companions [in Medina] numbered in the tens of thousands, but during the days of tribulation (*fitna*) [this number was] only decreased by forty or so men [who went into retreat].[67]

---

64 *Ṭūmār*, pl. *ṭawāmīr*, a journal, or a Persian term meaning a lengthy book or speech.

65 Trans. note: al-Zabīdī writes that this occurred after the death of ʿAlī b. Abī Ṭālib who was supported by many of the people in Kufa during the civil war with Muʿāwiya. The Kufans wrote to Ḥusayn and pledged their allegiance to him. Ibn ʿUmar and other Companions warned him that the Kufans would betray him just as they betrayed his father ʿAlī. Al-Zabīdī, *Itḥāf*, 6:355.

66 Al-Ājurī (d. 360/970), *al-Sharīʿa*, 1668; al-Khaṭṭābī, *al-ʿUzla*, 25. Al-Ghazālī used this latter narration.

67 Al-Khaṭṭābī, *al-ʿUzla*, 19, as a statement of Ibn Sīrīn رَحِمَهُ ٱللَّهُ.

Ṭāwūs [b. Kaysān] stayed [in retreat] in his house. When he was questioned about it, he said, "[It is because of] the corruption of the time and the oppression of the leaders."[68]

When ʿUrwa [b. al-Zubayr] built his fortress in al-ʿAqīq, he stayed in it. [Someone] said to him,

> "You stay in [your] fortress and abandon the mosque of the Messenger of God صلى الله عليه وسلم?"
>
> [ʿUrwa] said, "I see that your mosques are places of idle talk and your markets [are full of] false speech. Obscenity has ascended to your mountain roads, while [in my fortress] I am safe from what you engage in."[69]

So one of the benefits of retreat is protection from controversies and the consequences of tribulations.

The fourth benefit [of retreat]: Freedom from the evil of people.

They will harm you at one time by backbiting, at another time with evil thoughts and suspicion, and another time with expectations and deceitful demands that are difficult to fulfill. Yet again, [they will harm you] with slander and lies. Perhaps they see from your actions or statements what they do not fully understand. Then they store that away, saving it for a time when an opportunity for
evil appears. So, | when you separate from them, you are free from 290
having to protect yourself from all [their harm]. [About] this, one wise man said to another, "Shall I teach you two verses that are better than ten thousand dirhams?" He said, "What are they?" He said,

> Lower [your] voice when you speak at night,
> And turn about in the day before uttering a word;
>
> There is no return for a statement once said,
> Whether it is vile or good.[70]

---

68 Al-Khaṭṭābī, *al-ʿUzla*, 26.

69 Al-Khaṭṭābī, *al-ʿUzla*, 28; and Ibn ʿAbd al-Barr, *Jāmiʿ bayān al-ʿilm wa-faḍlih*, 2403.

70 Al-Khaṭṭābī, *al-ʿUzla*, 65. See also Ibn Abī l-Ḥadīd, *Sharḥ nahj al-balāgha*, 10:48. Trans. note: al-Zabīdī explains that one should speak softly at night because someone might overhear the conversation and use it against him later. Act as if the walls have ears. During the day be aware of your surroundings because someone who dislikes you might be listening. Once you make a statement you can never take it back, so beware of saying something you might regret later. Al-Zabīdī, *Itḥāf*, 6:356.

There is no doubt that if someone interacts with people, he will share in their actions. He cannot fully sever ties with an envious person and an enemy [who has] evil thoughts about him. He fantasizes that he could prepare [to defend] himself against aggressions, the burdensome plots against him, and the hidden calamities that follow. When people have intense desire for a matter, ...*they think that every shout is against them. They are the enemy, so beware of them*... [Q. 63:4].

When [people] have an intense desire for this world, they think that others also have that desire. Al-Mutanabbī said,

> When the actions of a man are evil, his thoughts are evil,
> And when he verifies suspicion with his daily practice;
>
> And he becomes an enemy to the one he loves with words of his enemies,
> Then he awakens in the night overshadowed by doubt.[71]

It was said, "Associating with evil [people] causes evil thoughts about the pious."[72] |

291 A person might encounter [many] types of evil from acquaintances and the many others with whom he interacts. We cannot elaborate on all the details. What we have mentioned indicates the scope of [these evils]. In retreat is freedom from all of them. Many people who have chosen retreat point to this. Thus Abū l-Dardāʾ said, "Test them, and you will hate them."[73]

A poet said,

> The one who praised people without testing them,
> Then tested them, blamed the one he praised
>
> Through solitude he became socially [desirable],
> Near and distant relatives grieved over his [absence].[74]

---

71 Al-ʿUkbarī, *Sharḥ Dīwān al-Mutanabbī*, 4:135; al-Ghazālī uses the verses from al-Mutanabbī in the same context that al-Khaṭṭābī used them. See al-Khaṭṭābī, *al-ʿUzla*, 40.

72 Al-Khaṭṭābī, *al-ʿUzla*, 40.

73 Ibn al-Mubārak, *al-Zuhd*, 185, and al-Khaṭṭābī, *al-ʿUzla*, 86. This means that if someone tests people, he will get to know them. Then he will come to hate them and leave them.

74 Al-Washāʾ, *al-Mawshā*, 22.

ʿUmar [b. al-Khaṭṭāb] رَضِيَٱللَّهُعَنْهُ said, "In retreat, there is rest from socializing with [an] evil [companion]."[75]

It was said to ʿAbdallāh [b. ʿUrwa] b. al-Zubayr, "Why will you not come to Medina?" He said, "Nothing remains there except [those who] envy the wealth of others and those [who find] joy in revenge."[76]

Ibn al-Sammāk said, "Our companion wrote, 'As for what follows: People are like a remedy used to treat oneself. Then they become a disease for which there is no cure. So flee from them as if fleeing from a lion.'"[77] |

One of the Bedouin took special care of a tree. He used to say, 292
"He is a beneficial companion (*nadīm*) with three qualities. If he hears something from me, he does not slander me. If I spit in his face, he tolerates that from me. And if I annoy him, he does not get angry." When [the caliph Hārūn] al-Rashīd heard that, he said, "I limited myself to beneficial companions."[78]

Another [Bedouin] was attached to books and graves. He was asked about this and said, "I have never known anything more peaceful than solitude, or more of an admonishment than a grave, or more delightful than a book as a companion."[79]

Ḥasan [al-Baṣrī] رَحِمَهُٱللَّهُ said,

> "I intend to go on pilgrimage."
>
> Thābit al-Banānī, who was one of the saints of God عَزَّوَجَلَّ, heard that and said, "It has come to me that you intend to go on pilgrimage. I would love for us to go as companions."
>
> Ḥasan said to him, "Woe to you! Let us go together with the veil of God over us. I fear for our companionship [because] one of us might see from the other what will cause us to hate each other."[80]

This indicates another benefit of retreat; it maintains a veil over the *dīn*, valor (*murūʾa*), [good] manners, destitution (*faqr*), and the

75 Ibn Abī Shayba, *al-Muṣannaf*, 35618; and al-Khaṭṭābī, *al-ʿUzla*, 13.

76 Al-Khaṭṭābī, *al-ʿUzla*, 29; and Abū Nuʿaym, *Ḥilya*, 7:299.

77 Al-Khaṭṭābī, *al-ʿUzla*, 35. The complete statement ends with "So take God تَعَالَىٰ for companionship and peace."

78 Al-Khaṭṭābī, *al-ʿUzla*, 44.

79 Al-Khaṭṭābī, *al-ʿUzla*, 27.

80 Al-Dīnawarī, *al-Majālisa wa-jawāhir al-ʿilm*, 201.

rest of the faults (ʿ*awrāt*). God سُبْحَانَهُ praises those who maintain a veil [over these aspects] when He says, . . . *An ignorant [person] would think them self-sufficient because of their restraint* . . . [Q. 2:273].

A poet[81] said,

> It is not a shame if the blessing of a free man ceases,
> Rather it is a shame if [his] embellishment ceases. |

293 No person is without faults in his *dīn*, his life, his manners, and his actions. The priority is for him to cover [his faults] in the *dīn* and worldly [actions]. There is no safety if it is uncovered.

Abū l-Dardāʾ said, "People used to be like roses without thorns. Today, they are like thorns without roses."[82] If this was the judgment in his time, in the latter decades of the first century [AH/seventh century CE], then these later times are undoubtedly more evil.

Sufyān b. ʿUyayna said, "Sufyān al-Thawrī said to me while he was alive and after his death in [my] dream, 'Limit [your knowledge of people [by association with them], for being free from them is difficult. I do not think that I have seen what I disliked except from those I knew.'"[83]

Someone said, "I went to Mālik b. Dīnār while he was sitting by himself. When a dog put its jaws on his knee, I moved to chase it away. He said, 'Leave it, O so-and-so. It is causing no harm or injury. It is better than sitting with an evil [person].'"[84]

It was said to someone, "What makes you withdraw from people?" He said, "I fear that I would lose my *dīn* without being aware [of it]."[85] |

294 This indicates that [a person's] disposition takes on the characteristics of an evil friend.

Abū l-Dardāʾ said, "Fear God and beware of people. They do not ride on the back of a camel except that they pierce it, nor on

81 The verse is attributed to ʿAlī b. al-Jahm (d. 249/863), *Dīwān*, 173.

82 Ibn Abī l-Dunyā, *Mudārāt al-nās*, 13. Trans. note: al-Zabīdī states that Abū l-Dardāʾ died in the year 32/652 or 653. Al-Zabīdī, *Itḥāf*, 6:358.

83 Al-Thawrī's statement while [Ibn. ʿUyayna] was awake was reported by Abū Nuʿaym, *Ḥilya*, 6:389, from Khalaf b. Tamīm. He also reported a similar statement about the dream; see Abū Nuʿaym, *Ḥilya*, 6:383.

84 Abū Nuʿaym, *Ḥilya*, 2:384.

85 Ibn al-Mubārak, *al-Zuhd*, 16, from the addendum of Nuʿaym b. Ḥammād. The statement is attributed to Sharaḥbīl b. al-Samṭ.

the back of a horse except that they wound it, nor on the heart of a believer except that they ruin it."

Someone said, "Limit your acquaintances, for that is safer for your *dīn* and your heart. It [also] lightens the duties that fall on you."[86] [This is true] because the more acquaintances you have, the more duties you have and the more difficult it is to fulfill them.

Someone said, "Disavow the one you know, and do not [get to] know those you do not know."[87]

The fifth benefit [of retreat]: It cuts off people's desire for you and your desire for people.

As for cutting off the desires of people, in that is every benefit. Pleasing people is an unattainable goal, so a person's priority [should be] preoccupation with improving himself.

Among the easiest and simplest duties are attending funeral prayers, visiting the sick, and attending wedding banquets and ceremonies (*al-walāʿim wa-l-amlākāt*), [but fulfilling these duties] includes wasting time and exposing [oneself] to harms.

[One] might be prevented from some of [these duties] by some
hindrance. Yet it is not possible | to present every excuse. [People] 295
would then say to him, "You fulfilled [lit., executed] the right of so-and-so, but you curtailed our right." That could become a cause of enmity. It is said that if someone does not visit the sick during the time of visitation, [it means that] he desires [the sick person's] death, and fears the shame of his neglect should he recover.

Whoever withdraws from all people—every one of them—all of them will be pleased with him, but if he prefers some over others, they [the others] will become estranged [from him]. One is not able to universally [give] them all [their] rights, even if he [spends] all day and night. What about one who is preoccupied with matters of *dīn* and the world?

ʿAmr b. al-ʿĀṣ said, "An increase in friends is an increase in creditors."[88]

---

86 Abū Ṭālib al-Makkī, *Qūt al-qulūb,* 2:213.

87 Abū Ṭālib al-Makkī, *Qūt al-qulūb,* 2:214.

88 Trans. note: There is no source mentioned for this narration. Al-Zabīdī says it means that the more friends one has, the more demands are put on him to fulfill their rights. Al-Zabīdī, *Itḥāf,* 6:359.

Ibn al-Rūmī[89] said,

> Your enemy benefits from your friend,
> So do not have many companions
>
> For surely the disease is more than what you see,
> It is from your food and drink.

Al-Shāfiʿī رَضِيَ اللَّهُ عَنْهُ said, "The origin of all enmity is the transformation of [what is] noble into [what is] ignoble."[90]

As for cutting off your desire for others, it also has ample benefit. If one looks to the beauty of this world and its adornment, his eagerness for it [will] increase, and his desire will grow according to the strength of his eagerness. And if he only sees disappointment in most desires, then he will be harmed by them. When he withdraws
296 [from people], he does not | witness [worldly adornment] and when he does not witness it, he does not yearn [for it] and desire it. And about this God تَعَالَىٰ says, *Do not extend your eyes toward that by which We have given enjoyment to [certain] categories of the disbelievers...* [Q. 15:88].

[The Prophet] صَلَّى اللَّهُ عَلَيْهِ وَسَلَّمَ said, "Look to the one who is beneath you and do not look to the one who is above you. It is not suitable to scorn the bounty God [gave] you."[91]

ʿAwn b. ʿAbdallāh said, "I used to sit with the wealthy, but I never ceased to be saddened. I would see a garment more beautiful than my garment and a horse more agile than my horse. Then I sat with the poor, and I became content."[92]

It has been said that al-Muzanī رَحِمَهُ اللَّهُ went out from the gate of the [congregational] mosque in Fusṭāṭ[93] and came across Ibn ʿAbd al-Ḥakam with his entourage. He was amazed by what he saw of [Ibn ʿAbd al-Ḥakam's] status and the beauty of his appearance. So he recited the verse of God تَعَالَىٰ, *...and We have made some of you [people] as [a] trial for others—will you have patience?* [Q. 25:20].

---

89 Ibn al-Rūmī (d. 283/896), *Dīwān*, 1:231.

90 Al-Khaṭṭābī reported something similar in *al-ʿUzla*, 94. The wording given here is from Abū Nuʿaym, *Ḥilya*, 6:390, as a statement of Sufyān al-Thawrī رَحِمَهُ اللَّهُ.

91 Muslim, *Ṣaḥīḥ*, 2963.

92 Al-Khaṭṭābī, *al-ʿUzla*, 35; Abū Nuʿaym, *Ḥilya*, 4:243.

93 Fusṭāṭ was the first capital of Egypt under the Umayyads and ʿAbbāsids; it was located on the eastern bank of the Nile, south of modern Cairo.

Then he said, "Indeed, I will be patient and pleased." He was a poor man of little means.[94]

One who is [secluded] in his house is not tested with these
tribulations. One who witnesses the adornment of this world [has
two options]; he [can] strengthen his *dīn* and his certainty, and be
patient, [and in this] he must repeatedly swallow the [bitter] medicine
of patience, which is more bitter [than taking medicine once]. Or,
[he can let] his yearning [for this world] grow, and deceitfully strive
for this world and [it will] destroy him completely and permanently.
As for this world, [destruction] from desire causes ruin most of
the time because not everyone | who seeks this world has an easy
time [attaining it]. As for the hereafter, [destruction] comes from 297
choosing the pleasantness of this world over the remembrance of
God تعالى and drawing near Him.

On this, Ibn al-ʿArābī said,

> If the gate of humiliation is from the stance of riches
> Then I will rise to dignity from the stance of poverty.[95]

This indicates that desire causes a state of humiliation.

The sixth benefit [of retreat]: Freedom from witnessing disagreeable [people] (*thuqalāʾ*) and fools, and enduring the foolishness of their ways and manners.

Seeing a disagreeable [person] is the lesser blindness.

It was said to al-Aʿmash, "What brings tears to your eyes?" He said, "Looking at disagreeable [people]."[96]

It was said that Abū Ḥanīfa came to al-Aʿmash and said to him,

---

94 Al-Khaṭṭābī, *al-ʿUzla*, 35. Trans. note: Ismāʿīl b. Yaḥyā l-Muzanī was a student of al-Shāfiʿī, and was known as one of the great ascetics of his time. The congregational mosque in Fusṭāṭ, Egypt, is named after the Companion ʿAmr b. al-ʿĀṣ. Ibn ʿAbd al-Ḥakam was an extremely wealthy and pompous man. Al-Zabīdī, *Itḥāf*, 6:360.

95 Al-Khaṭṭābī, *al-ʿUzla*, 36.

96 Al-Khaṭṭābī, *al-ʿUzla*, 42. Trans. note: al-Aʿmash is Sulaymān b. Mihrān (d. 147 or 148/764 or 765). He saw some of the Companions but is not considered a Follower (*tābiʿī*). Al-Zabīdī, *Itḥāf*, 6:361.

> In a report (*khabar*) it states that if God takes away someone's eyes (*karīmatayh*), then God will replace them with what is better.[97]
>
> "What has He given you as a replacement?"
>
> He said in a jestful manner, "The replacement He gave me for them is that it is sufficient for me to recognize the lazy, and you are one of them.[98] |

298 Ibn Sīrīn said, "I heard a man say, 'I looked at a lazy [person] once, and I lost consciousness.'"[99]

Jālīnūs said, "Everything has a prohibited [element], and the prohibited [element] of the spirit (*rūḥ*) is looking at lazy [people]."[100]

Al-Shāfiʿī رضي الله عنه said, "I did not sit next to a lazy [person] except that I found the side of my body next to him feeling heavier than the other side."

Except for the first two, these [six] benefits [of retreat] are associated with goals related to current worldly matters, but they can also be applied to the *dīn*. However much someone is harmed by looking at a lazy person, he cannot be safe from backbiting [against] him and disapproving of what God produced [i.e., the lazy person]. Then when he is harmed by someone's backbiting, or suspicions, or by being envied, or from slander, etc., he will not be able to restrain himself from [wanting] compensation (*mukāfāʾ*).[101] All of that leads to the corruption of the *dīn*. In retreat, there is safety from all of that, so understand [this].

---

97 Al-Bukhārī, *Ṣaḥīḥ*, 5653, reported the following as attributed to the Prophet صلى الله عليه وسلم, "God said, 'When I test My servant concerning his eyes (*ḥabībatayh*), and he is patient, I will give him paradise as a replacement for them.'"

98 Ibn ʿAdī, *al-Kāmil*, 6:325; Ibn ʿAbd al-Barr, *Jāmiʿ bayān al-ʿilm wa-faḍlih*, 2164. See also al-Zabīdī, *Itḥāf*, 6:361.

99 Al-Khaṭṭābī, *al-ʿUzla*, 43.

100 Al-Khaṭṭābī, *al-ʿUzla*, 43, from al-Aʿmash, from Jālīnūs. Trans. note: Jālīnūs is the Arabized spelling of Galen, who was a second-century CE Greek physician and philosopher. Al-Aʿmash is transmitting from translated sources. See Walzer, "D̲j̲ālīnūs," *EI²* 2:402–403.

101 Ed. note: this is a euphemism for retaliation.

[3]

The Harms of Retreat 299

KNOW that among the religious (*dīniyya*) and worldly (*dunyawiyya*) goals is bringing benefit by helping others, and that is attained only through socializing. Everything that brings benefit through socializing is absent in retreat, and this absence is one of the harms of retreat.

So you must look at the benefits and requirements of socializing. What are they? They are teaching and learning; benefiting others and receiving benefits; teaching and learning good manners; being sociable and acting sociably; attaining reward for oneself and others by fulfilling [their] rights; becoming accustomed to humility; and gaining experience by witnessing various states and learning from them.

Now we will explain this. There are seven benefits of socializing.

The first benefit: Teaching and learning

We have mentioned the virtue of these two actions in *Kitāb al-ʿilm*.[1] These are two of the greatest [acts of] worship in this world and can only be realized by socializing. The [fields of] knowledge are numerous; some of them are recommended while others are necessary in this world.

Thus, when [knowledge] is incumbent on him, the one in need of learning becomes disobedient by retreating. If one has learned the obligations, and is not predisposed to delving into the [religious]

---

1 Book 1 of the *Revival of the Religious Sciences: The Book of Knowledge*.

sciences because he views himself to be preoccupied with worship, [then he] can withdraw [from society].

If he is capable of expanding [his knowledge] in the legal and
300 rational sciences, then retreat prior to | learning is the utmost loss. And about this, al-Nakhaʿī and others said, "Study jurisprudence, then withdraw."[2]

The one who withdraws before learning, in most cases, wastes his time sleeping or thinking about foolish things. His goal is to spend his time [reciting] litanies with comprehension. Yet in his physical and spiritual actions he continues to engage in various types of deception, so his efforts are ruined and his [good] acts are negated without him even knowing it. In his convictions about God and His attributes, he continues to [have] illusions and become accustomed to them. He has corrupt thoughts that afflict him and in most of his states he is [an object of] laughter for Satan, [even though] he sees himself as among the worshipers.

Since knowledge is the foundation of the *dīn*, it is not good for the common folk and the ignorant [to go into] retreat. By this I mean those who are unable to perfect worship in retreat and [who] do not know everything that is necessary for [worship].

The example of the soul is the example of a sick person in need of a caring physician to heal him. The ignorant sick person, when he cuts himself off from a doctor before becoming knowledgeable in medicine, will without doubt worsen his illness. Thus, retreat is only fitting for knowledgeable people.

Teaching contains a great reward when the intentions of the teacher and student are sound. When the goal is to establish rank and to increase companions and followers, then it destroys the *dīn*. We have mentioned aspects of this in *Kitāb al-ʿilm*.[3]

In this time, the judgment of the scholar is that one can retreat if he desires to safeguard his *dīn* and if he cannot find [a sincere student] seeking [spiritual] benefit in his *dīn*. But the only student
301 [found now seeks] embellished speech, by which he lures | the common folk in public [lit., exhibitions of] admonitions, or complex

---

2 Al-Khaṭṭābī, *al-ʿUzla*, 42.

3 Trans. note: For further discussion on the dangers of seeking religious knowledge for worldly purposes, see al-Ghazālī, *Kitāb al-ʿilm: The Book of Knowledge*, 170–190.

disputations, by which he aims to silence those around him and draw near the sultan. He applies [himself] in exhibitions of rivalry and boastfulness.

[The student] draws near the coveted knowledge of [his] legal school (*madhhab*),[4] mainly seeking a means to approach exemplary scholars, to act in an authoritative capacity, and to gain wealth. Thus the requirements of both the *dīn* and prudence call for withdrawal from [all of these students].

So if one finds a student [who seeks knowledge for the sake] of God and [seeks] to draw near God with knowledge, then one of the greatest of the major sins is to withdraw from [this student] and withhold knowledge from him. One does not find more than one or two such students, even in a large city, if they can be found at all.

A person should not be deceived by the statement of Sufyān [al-Thawrī], "We gained knowledge for other than [the sake of] God, but knowledge can only be for the sake of God."[5] Thus the jurists (*fuqahāʾ*) sought knowledge for other than [the sake of] God. Then they returned to God. Just look at the last years of most of their lives and learn (*ʿitibār*) from them. They died while they were in a state of ruin [for] seeking this life (*ṭalab al-dunyā*) and assailing [each other] over it. Or, they turned away from [this life] and [became] ascetics. [Hearing] information (*khabar*)[6] is not the same as observation.[7]

Know that the knowledge that Sufyān is referring to [in his statement] is knowledge of *ḥadīth*, commentary (*tafsīr*) on the Qurʾān,

---

4 This refers to matters associated with his school of thought. Al-Zabīdī, *Itḥāf*, 6:363. This may refer specifically to jurisprudence (*fiqh*). Al-Ghazālī indicates that his purpose in writing the *Iḥyāʾ* was to heal hearts. Trans. note: In this section of the *Itḥāf*, al-Zabīdī further defines the motivations of such a scholar. Thus, what is translated as "to act in an authoritative capacity" (*tawallī l-wilāyāt*), al-Zabīdī explains as giving rulings (*iftāʾ*) and judgments (*qaḍāʾ*), being with the leaders of schools, and speaking with prominent [spiritual] orators.

5 Al-Ghazālī explained the meaning of this in another of his works, *Mīzān al-ʿamal*, 343.

6 Ed. note: In this instance, *khabar* refers to knowledge or information. An English equivalent of this aphorism might be "hearing is not the same as seeing."

7 Trans. note: al-Zabīdī mentions that this last statement (*laysa al-khabar ka-l-muʿāyana*) is a *ḥadīth* attributed to the Prophet ﷺ, and he gave all the chains of narrators for it. Al-Zabīdī, *Itḥāf*, 6:363.

and knowledge of the biographies of the prophets and Companions. In these [we find] cautionary [information] and warnings that will
302 cause [someone] | to fear God. So even if [this knowledge] does not have an immediate effect, it [will] have an effect later.

Dialectic theology (*kalām*) and basic jurisprudence [used in] association with practical rulings and the resolution of disputations have an established opinion (*madhhab*) and a dissenting opinion (*khilāf*). These will not cause the one who desires [this knowledge] for the purpose of this world to return to God تَعَالَىٰ; rather, he will continue to persist in error until the end of his life according to [the extent of] his eagerness.

Perhaps what we have laid out in this book, if the student [who] desires this world studies it, [will] allow him to return [to God, if not now], then [we] hope he will [accept] this reproach at the end of his life. He would then be filled with the fear of God, desire for the hereafter, and wariness of this world. That [reproach] is found in the *ḥadīth* and commentary (*tafsīr*) on the Qurʾān, it is not found in dialectic theology, dissenting [opinions], or in [established] opinion. A person should not deceive himself. The restrained scholar [is in a] happier condition in his restraint than is the deluded ignorant [person] or one who is deceived by his own opinions.

Each scholar [who is] intensely eager to teach is always at risk that his purpose [may really] be for acceptance and status, and in that case his fortune may delight him [lit., his *nafs*, when he] senses [that he can] argue and overcome the ignorant. Thus, the harm of knowledge is self-conceit, as [the Prophet] صَلَّى ٱللَّٰهُ عَلَيْهِ وَسَلَّمَ said.[8]

And [about] this, it was reported from Bishr [b. al-Ḥārith al-Ḥāfī] that he buried seventeen crates of books of *ḥadīth* that he heard [from his teachers]. He did not relate [*ḥadīth*], but he would say, "I
303 desire to relate [*ḥadīth*], so for that reason | I do not relate [*ḥadīth*]. If I desired not to relate [*ḥadīth*], I would relate [*ḥadīth*]."[9]

---

8 This is well known, as al-ʿIrāqī said. There is a *ḥadīth*, "The danger of knowledge is forgetfulness, and the danger of beauty is self-conceit." This is part of a longer *ḥadīth* reported by al-Bayhaqī, *Shuʿab al-īmān*, 4326. See al-Zabīdī, *Itḥāf*, 6:364.

9 Abū Ṭālib al-Makkī, *Qūt al-qulūb*, 1:156. Something similar was reported by al-Khaṭīb al-Baghdādī (d. 463/1070 or 1071), *Sharaf aṣḥāb al-ḥadīth*, 230.

And [about] this he also said, "Saying, 'He narrated to us,' is one of the gates to this world. When a man says, 'He narrated to us,' he is only saying, 'They have made me rich.'"[10]

Rābiʿa al-ʿAdawiyya said to Sufyān al-Thawrī, "What a good man you are! If only your desire was not for this world." He said, "What do I desire?" She said, "[to relate] *ḥadīth*."[11]

And [about] this, Abū Sulaymān al-Dārānī said, "Whoever marries, compiling *ḥadīth*, or is busy traveling, has put his trust in this world [instead of God]."[12]

We have brought attention to these harms in *Kitāb al-ʿilm*. In retreat, [one should be] determined and vigilant, and leave many [lit., excessive] companions as much as possible. Whoever seeks this world in his studies and his teaching, the correct response to him, if one is rational (*ʿāqil*), is to abandon him, especially in times like these. Abū Sulaymān al-Khaṭṭābī certainly spoke the truth when he said,

> Leave [those who] desire to be your companions and [those who] learn from you, for there is neither wealth nor beauty for you from them. They are brothers publicly but enemies in secret. When they meet with you, they show affection to you, and when they are absent from you, they disparage you. 304
> Whoever comes to you | observes you, and when he leaves, he talks about you [i.e., your faults]. [They are] people of hypocrisy, slander, malevolence, and deceit. So do not be deceived by their companionship with you. Their goal in [attaining] knowledge is only for status and wealth. They take you as a means for their aims and objectives and as a donkey for their needs.
>
> If you are remiss concerning [the achievement of] their goals, they will be your bitter enemy. They consider their repeated visits to you as evidence against you, for they view it as a right and obligation from you to them. They oblige you to

10 Abū Ṭālib al-Makkī, *Qūt al-qulūb*, 1:135.

11 Abū Ṭālib al-Makkī, *Qūt al-qulūb*, 2:57. Trans. note: al-Zabīdī explains that Rābiʿa was criticizing his fame as a *ḥadīth* scholar because people longed to study with him and she was concerned that this might lead to arrogance or character defects. Al-Zabīdī, *Itḥāf*, 6:364.

12 Abū Ṭālib al-Makkī, *Qūt al-qulūb*, 1:135.

> act liberally toward them with your honor, your status, and your *dīn*. Thus, [they expect] you to be an enemy to their enemies and a supporter of their associates. You are to serve them and protect them. You stand before them as a fool when once you were jurist (*faqīh*). You have become a contemptible follower to them, after you were a prominent leader. And [about] this it is said, "Withdrawal from the common folk is perfect valor (*murūʾa*)."[13]

This is the intent of [Abū Sulaymān al-Khaṭṭābī's] statement, and even though it differs from some of his [exact] expressions, it is true and correct. You will see teachers constantly serving and necessarily obligated and burdened by favors they [must] give to those who come to them repeatedly. It is as if [the student] is giving them a gift, for he sees it as his right [to learn from the teachers] and as an obligation on them. Perhaps he does not come frequently to [a teacher] so as not to be liable for [his teacher's] provisions in any amount [at all]. Then the poor teacher might weaken in order to [acquire] wealth for himself. He must continue to go to the gates of the sultans, suffer disgrace, and feel the distress of suffering degradation and submission. This continues until he is fated to take prohibited money through illegal means. He then continues to work in servitude and service to [a patron] who forces [him] to work and submit, such that he surrenders to [his patron] the repeated favors he is able to offer him. And among his peers he
305 continues to endure a low status. | If he is equal among them, those who surpass him hate him. They accuse him of foolishness, lack of discernment, and failing to attain an outpouring of favor and [failing to] establish measures of truth with justice. If he avoids them, the fools disparage him with sharp tongues. They rise up against him like vipers and lions. So he continues to suffer from [the fools] in this world and in the end [hereafter] from the sins he committed taking and dispersing [prohibited wealth].

It is amazing that with all these trials, [the teacher's] soul still indulges in falsehoods and clings to deception. [His soul] says to

13 This is the statement of al-Khaṭṭābī, *al-ʿUzla*, 39.

him,[14] Do not be remiss in your efforts. You are doing this only as one seeking the face of God تَعَالَىٰ, promulgating the laws (*sharʿ*) of the Messenger of God صَلَّى ٱللَّهُ عَلَيْهِ وَسَلَّمَ, publicizing knowledge of the *dīn* of God, and establishing a sufficient number of students of knowledge from among the worshipers of God. The wealth [I take] of the sultans has no real possessor and should be made ready for the public good. And what good is greater than increasing the number of scholars? For it is through them that the *dīn* is made known and its people are strengthened.

If only he were not the object of Satan's ridicule, he would know with minimal consideration that the corruption of the time is only caused by the increase of jurists (*fuqahāʾ*). [They are] like those who devour whatever they find, without distinguishing between the allowable and the prohibited. The eyes of the ignorant are on them, and [the ignorant] become bold in committing sins based on the boldness of [corrupt scholars]. [The ignorant] imitate them and imitate their examples. And [about] this it is said, "People do not become corrupt except through the corruption of the leaders. The leaders do not become corrupt except through the corruption of the scholars (*ʿulamāʾ*)." Thus we seek refuge with God from deception and blindness, for it is a disease that has no cure. |

The second benefit [of socializing]: Giving and receiving benefits 306

Receiving benefits from other people comes through earning [a living] and mutual interactions, and that can only be attained through socializing. One in need of that must abandon retreat. So he [may] enter into the struggle (*jihād*) of socializing, if seeking this is in accordance with the law, as we mentioned in *Kitāb* [*ādāb*] *al-kasab*.[15]

If one is convinced that what he has is sufficient for him, he is content. So retreat is better for him if most of the ways of earning a living are closed to him, [and] only those [that necessitate] disobedience [remain]. Unless his goal is to earn [enough to give]

---

14 Trans. note: The Minhāj edition has *taqūl lahu* (lit., "his soul says to him") and the *Itḥāf* has *yaqūl lahā* (lit., "he says to his soul"). Al-Zabīdī states that the different expressions reflect the perspective of his soul speaking to him or of him speaking to his soul. Al-Zabīdī, *Itḥāf*, 6:366.

15 Book 13 of the *Revival of the Religious Sciences: The Proprieties of Acquisition and Earning a Living*.

charity. So if he earns from a [valid] source and [gives in] charity, it is better than retreat. Preoccupation with supererogatory deeds (*nāfila*) is not better than retreat; preoccupation with realizing gnosis of God تَعَالَىٰ and knowledge of legal sciences [is better], and reaching the essence of eagerness [to know] God تَعَالَىٰ solely for the remembrance of God [is better]. That is, whoever attains familiarity with intimate discourse with God through unveilings and insight, and not through delusions and false fantasies [benefits most].

As for benefiting [others]: One benefits people with his wealth or his person; he stands on the path of reward [from God] by [fulfilling] their needs, for there is reward in rising to fulfill the needs of Muslims and this can only be achieved through socializing. If one is able [to partake in socializing], while maintaining the boundaries of the law, then that is preferable over retreat, especially if his preoccupation in retreat is [limited to] voluntary prayers and other physical acts of worship. If the path of the actions of the heart is opened for him through his constant remembrance and reflection, then nothing is equivalent to that. |

307 **The third benefit**: Teaching and learning [good] manners

By [learning good manners] we mean training [oneself] to endure people and to struggle to bear their harm through breaking [the evil inclinations of] the soul and conquering desires. This is among the benefits one acquires by socializing. [Socializing] is preferable to retreat for anyone who has not corrected his manners and whose desires are not in obedience to the boundaries of the law.

The servants of the Sufis in the hospices (*rabāṭ*) are commissioned to interact with people to serve them and the people of the market can [make] requests of them. [This is meant] to break the soul's thoughtlessness and to draw on the blessed supplications of the Sufis who focus their attention on God سُبْحَانَهُ.

This was the origin [of hospices] in past times. Today, corrupt goals have been mixed [with their original purpose]. That [corruption] is opposed to the laws [regulating hospices] just as the rest of the rites of the *dīn* are opposed [to corruption]. What began as seeking humility through service became an insistence on increasing followers, a means to gather wealth, and a way to gain assistance by [obtaining] numerous followers. If this is the intention [of Sufis

in hospices], then retreat is better than that, even to the grave. If training the soul is the intention, then it is better than retreat for one in need of training. This is an aspect of what is necessary at the beginning of one's decision [to train the soul]. After the attainment of training, it is fitting to understand [by analogy] that a trained animal is not always sought for that for which it was trained. Rather, the intent is for [the riding animal] to take the rider to pass through stages so the journey | is covered quickly. As such, the body is the 308
riding animal for the heart. [The heart] rides [the body] for the journey on the road to the hereafter. The body has desires, and if [the person] does not break them, they will overcome him on the road, leading him astray. One who occupies [himself] his whole life with training is like one who occupies himself his whole life training a riding animal but then never rides it. There is no benefit to [this riding animal] except that [one] is free from a situation in which the animal bites or kicks. By my life, this is an intended benefit, but it could also be attained from a dead beast! The intended purpose of a riding animal is to attain benefit from it while it is alive. Likewise, there is freedom from the pain of desires in a state of sleep or death, but it is not suitable for one to be content with this. This is like one who addresses a monk (*rāhib*), saying, "O monk," and he responds, saying, "I am not a monk. I am a rapacious dog, and I have confined myself until I will no longer attack people."[16] This is good in relation to the one who attacks people. But it is not suitable to limit him [the monk] to this [description]; one who kills himself also does not attack people. Rather, it is suitable to seek the utmost [goal] intended. Whoever understands this and is guided to the path and is capable of the journey, then it will become clear to him that retreat is more helpful than socializing. Thus, the most virtuous course for someone like this is to first engage in socializing, and then retreat.

As for teaching [good] manners, by this we mean only that he trains others. This is the condition of the shaykh of the Sufis in dealing with [the Sufis]. [The shaykh] is not capable of rectifying the [novices] except by socializing with them. [The shaykh's] condition is the condition of the teacher, and [his] ruling is like [the teacher's]

16 Trans. note: al-Zabīdī states that this narration was reported by Abū Nuʿaym in *Ḥilya* and al-Qushayrī in *al-Risāla*. See al-Zabīdī, *Itḥāf*, 6:367.

ruling. All types of specific harms and hypocrisy find their way to [the shaykh] while he transmits knowledge. The exception is that the [Sufi] novices who seek training are farther from [showing] signs of seeking this world than the seekers of knowledge [in traditional schools (*fī l-madāris*)].[17] And there are few [people] seen among [the
309 Sufi novices] while there are many [people] | among the seekers of [traditional] knowledge. So it is suitable to compare what is possible for [the shaykh] concerning seclusion with what is possible for [the shaykh] concerning socializing and improving people. [The shaykh] should accept one of the two [choices, seclusion or socializing] over the other. [He] should favor what is preferable [of the two choices], and that involves precise independent judgment that differs according to conditions and personalities. It is not possible for [us to make an] absolute judgment on [the shaykh] in terms of [whether the choice should be] negated or affirmed.

The fourth benefit: Companionability and intimacy

The goal of the one who attends wedding banquets, invitations, family get-togethers is companionability. According to the situation, this [benefit] refers to the lot of the soul (*nafs*). [Socializing] may be forbidden in some cases, when [one is] familiar with someone with whom he is not allowed to be familiar with, or [this] may be neutral and [in another case] it may be recommended; [in all cases it should be] in accord with the commandments of the *dīn*. One should consider this companionable [person] by observing his states and statements regarding the *dīn*, as [when one seeks to be] companionable with scholars who hold fast to the way of piety. This [issue of companionship] is associated with the lot of the soul, and is recommended when the goal is refreshing the heart in order to awaken motivation [toward] vigorous worship. Certainly, when hearts feel coerced, they become blind. Sometimes in solitude there is loneliness, and in gatherings there is sociability that refreshes the heart, and [these gatherings] are preferable. Gentleness in worship is part of resolute worship.[18]

---

17 Trans. note: al-Zabīdī distinguishes between novices (*murīdīn*) and traditional students of legal schools. Al-Zabīdī, *Itḥāf*, 6:368.

18 Ed. note: The concept of gentleness in worship is discussed in the next few *ḥadīth*s cited here. One should ease into worship by performing regular acts of worship and working toward those that require more physical stamina. If one starts off with

And [about] this, [the Prophet] صَلَّى ٱللَّهُ عَلَيْهِ وَسَلَّمَ said, "Indeed, God
does not become weary until you are weary."[19] | There is no escape 310
from this matter [of becoming weary], for the soul cannot remain constantly committed to the truth (*ḥaqq*) without being refreshed and pursuit of the commandment repulses [one out of weariness]. If one makes this *dīn* rigid, it will overwhelm him. The *dīn* is firm, and the custom of the insightful is to penetrate it with gentleness.[20]

And [about] this, Ibn ʿAbbās رَضِيَ ٱللَّهُ عَنْهُمَا said,

> "Were it not out of fear of the whispering (*waswās*) [of Satan], I would not sit with people." And once he said, "[Were it not out of fear of the whispering of Satan], I would only enter a city in which I had no known companion. Is not the corruption of people only by people?"[21]

One who has withdrawn can have a [close] companion with whom he is congenial, seeing him and talking with him for a time during the day and night. He must strive to find someone who will not corrupt him during these hours [they are together] and [bring ruin] for the remainder of his time [i.e., life]. [The Prophet] صَلَّى ٱللَّهُ عَلَيْهِ وَسَلَّمَ said, "A man [follows] the *dīn* of his intimate friend (*khalīl*), so each of you must consider the one with whom he forms an intimate friendship."[22]

He should be eager [to ensure] that the conversation when they meet is about the affairs of the *dīn* and discussing the states of the heart. [Conversation] should also be about his grievances and his shortcomings related to adherence to the truth and guidance to righteousness. In this there is invigoration and refreshment for the soul. It contains a broad scope for each person who is occupied with improving himself. There is no end to his grievances, even

---

physically strenuous acts of worship there is a danger that one might abondon all such worship. For example, a novice is discouraged from expending all his energy in superogatory night prayers that will exhaust him physically and leave him tired during the day and may lead him to miss obligatory prayers. This would then lead him to abandon night prayers and turn him away from prayer altogether.

19 Al-Bukhārī, *Ṣaḥīḥ*, 43, 1151; Muslim, *Ṣaḥīḥ*, 782, as part of a longer *ḥadīth*.

20 This is indicated in the *ḥadīth* of Anas رَضِيَ ٱللَّهُ عَنْهُ reported by Ibn Ḥanbal, *Musnad*, 11:77.

21 Ibn Abī l-Dunyā, *Mudārāt al-nās*, 126. His statement is also in Abū Ṭālib al-Makkī, *Qūt al-qulūb*, 2:142.

22 Abū Dāwūd, *Sunan*, 4833; al-Tirmidhī, *Sunan*, 2278.

if he were to live a long life. One who is pleased with himself is
311 certainly deceived.[23] |

This type of companionability for certain hours of the day might be preferable to retreat for some people. So he should first investigate the states of the heart and the states of the companion, and then sit with him.

The fifth benefit: Attaining reward for oneself and for others

As for attaining [benefit for oneself], this refers to attending funerals, visiting the sick, attending the two festivals (*ʿīdayn*), and without a doubt attending the Friday [congregational] prayer. It also refers to attending the rest of the prayers in congregation, for [one] is not allowed to miss them unless one fears a clear harm that is greater than losing the reward of the congregational [prayer] and its additional [benefits].[24] However, this [harm] happens only rarely. There is reward for attending weddings and [other] invitations because it brings joy to the heart of a Muslim.

As for benefiting others, this means leaving the door open for people to visit him [when he is sick], to console him during misfortune, or congratulate him for a blessing. Thus, [others] attain rewards through him. Likewise, if he is one of the scholars and permits people to visit him, they earn the reward of the visit while he was the cause enabling it.

It is now suitable to weigh the reward of these [cases of] socializing with the harms that we mentioned. Should retreat be given preference, or should socializing be given preference? It has been reported from a group of the predecessors, such as Mālik b. Anas and others, that they abandoned responding to invitations, visiting the sick, and attending funerals; moreover, they remained

---

23 Al-Zabīdī writes: [The one in retreat] does not mention anything concerning the affairs of this world, the states of corrupt people, grievances about oppressors, and what is widespread from the corrupt state of the common folk. Al-Zabīdī, *Itḥāf*, 6:369. Trans. note: al-Zabīdī clarifies that one should focus on himself and the inner states of his heart, not on outer circumstances.

24 Ed. note: This refers to the five prayers that men are encouraged to pray in a mosque; women are encouraged to perform these prayers privately, in the home. This should not be understood as an effort to keep women out of the public sphere or from engaging in other activites.

(*aḥlās*) in their homes.[25] They did not go out except for the Friday
[congregational prayer] and to visit graves. | Some of them left the 312
cities and ventured to remote areas of the mountains [in order to] focus on worship and flee from [worldly] concerns.

The sixth benefit of socializing: Humility

[Humility] is the most virtuous of the stations, and it is not possible in solitude.[26] It could be that arrogance is the reason for choosing retreat. It is reported in [the stories of] the Israelites (Isrāʾīliyyāt), that a wise man wrote three hundred sixty books about wisdom, so he thought he had attained a station (*manzil*) with God. So God تَعَالَىٰ revealed to His prophet,

> "Say to so-and-so, 'You have filled the earth with hypocrisy, and I accept nothing from your hypocrisy.'" [The wise man] then went into the country and stayed alone in a den underground, and said, "Now I have surely attained the pleasure of my Lord."
>
> So God تَعَالَىٰ revealed to His prophet, "Say to him, 'You have not attained My pleasure.'"
>
> Then [the wise man] went into the market places, and he socialized with the common folk and sat among them. He counseled them,[27] ate with them, and walked through the markets with them.
>
> So God تَعَالَىٰ revealed to His prophet, "Now you have attained My pleasure."[28]

There are many examples of a man withdrawing to his home, and his motivation is arrogance. He abstains from [interacting] with
people only because | he is not honored and held in esteem; or he 313
views socializing with disdain [and believes retreat] will elevate his status and preserve his high praise among people.

---

25 The word *aḥlās* is the plural of *ḥils*, which is a rough carpet laid on the ground, with a nicer carpet placed on top of it. This means that they stayed at home and did not go out, just as the *aḥlās* do not go out, and it indicates the perfection of humility (*tawāduʿ*). Al-Zabīdī, *Itḥāf*, 6:369.

26 This is because humility (*tawāduʿ*) requires the interaction of two people. Al-Zabīdī, *Itḥāf*, 6:370.

27 Ed. note: Or, "fed them, ate with them..."

28 Abū Ṭālib al-Makkī, *Qūt al-qulūb*, 2:233.

Perhaps he withdraws out of fear that [people] will see his faults if he socializes [with them]. One should not believe that he is an ascetic and focused on worship. He stays in his house as a cover for his faults, while perpetuating peoples' conviction about his asceticism and devotion, [but] without immersing [himself] in seclusion for remembrance and reflection.

The sign of these [people] is that they love to have others visit them, but they do not love to visit others. They are happy when people and rulers come to them, gathering at their doors and in their streets. They are happy when [people and rulers] take their hands to gain blessings. If he were [truly] preoccupied with [correcting] himself then he would hate socializing and visiting people, and he would also hate others visiting him. We mentioned al-Fuḍayl [b. ʿIyāḍ] who said, "Did you only come to me to so I can make you look good and you make me look good?"[29] And it was reported that Ḥātim al-Aṣamm said to the *amīr* that visited him, "My need is for me not to see you and for you not to see me."

If one is not occupying himself with the remembrance of God, then his withdrawal from people causes his preoccupation with people to intensify because his heart is merely turning to [their] view of him, [and he continues to desire their] honor and respect.

There are two aspects by which retreat is ignorance. [From] one aspect, humbleness and socializing do not diminish the eminence of one who has a high rank in his knowledge or his *dīn*. As such,
314 ʿAlī [b. Abī Ṭālib] رَضِيَ اللَّهُ عَنْهُ carried dates and salt in his garment | and with his hand, saying,[30]

> The perfection of the perfect [man] is not diminished
> by what he brings to benefit his family.

Abū Hurayra, Ḥudhayfa, Ubayy, and Ibn Masʿūd رَضِيَ اللَّهُ عَنْهُمْ used to carry bundles of wood and sacks of flour on their shoulders.[31]

Abū Hurayra رَضِيَ اللَّهُ عَنْهُ, when he was governor of Medina, [used to carry] wood on his head and say, "Make way for your *amīr*."[32]

---

29 Ibn Abī l-Dunyā, *al-ʿUzla wa-l-infirād*, 72.

30 Reported in ʿAlī b. Abī Ṭālib, *Dīwān*, 212.

31 Abū Ṭālib al-Makkī, *Qūt al-qulūb*, 2:233.

32 Al-Qushayrī, *al-Risāla*, 269.

The master of the messengers صَلَّى ٱللَّٰهُ عَلَيْهِ وَسَلَّمَ used to buy something and then carry it to his house himself. His Companion would say to him, "Give it to me and I will carry it." And he said, "The owner of a thing has more duty to carry it."[33]

Ḥasan b. ʿAlī رَضِيَ ٱللَّٰهُ عَنْهُمَا passed by some beggars who had scraps of bread. They said to him, "Come and eat, O [grand]son of the Messenger of God!" He dismounted and sat down on the road and ate with them. Then he mounted his riding animal and said, "God surely does not love the arrogant."[34] | 315

[**From**] **the second** aspect, one who occupies himself seeking to gain the pleasure of people and to improve their opinion of him is deceived, because if he were to know God with true knowledge, [he would know] that the creation cannot profit him in any way against God. [He would know] that the harm and benefit that comes to him is in the hand of God and there is no other benefit and harm but His. [He would also know] that if someone seeks the pleasure and love of people by angering God, then God will be angry with him, and people will be angry with him.[35] Moreover, attaining the pleasure of people is a goal that cannot be attained. Seeking the pleasure of God is foremost. [About] this al-Shāfiʿī رَضِيَ ٱللَّٰهُ عَنْهُ said to Yūnus b. ʿAbd al-Aʿlā, "By God, what I say to you is advice. There is no way to attain safety from people. So look to what improves you, and do that."[36]

[About] this it is said,[37]

> Whoever fears people will die grieving,
> And the courageous will succeed with delight.

---

33 Abū Yaʿlā (d. 307/919 or 920), *Musnad*, 6162; al-Ṭabarānī, *al-Muʿjam al-awsaṭ*, 6590. Abū Hurayra رَضِيَ ٱللَّٰهُ عَنْهُ asked to carry the trousers that the Prophet صَلَّى ٱللَّٰهُ عَلَيْهِ وَسَلَّمَ had bought for himself.

34 Trans. note: al-Zabīdī mentions that it is part of a longer narration that was reported in Abū Ṭālib al-Makkī, *Qūt al-qulūb*. Al-Zabīdī, *Itḥāf*, 6:371.

35 This is based on the meaning of a *ḥadīth* that was reported by al-Tirmidhī, *Sunan*, 2414, from ʿĀʾisha رَضِيَ ٱللَّٰهُ عَنْهَا as attributed to the Prophet صَلَّى ٱللَّٰهُ عَلَيْهِ وَسَلَّمَ, "If someone seeks the pleasure of God by angering people, then God will suffice him against the burden of the people. If someone seeks the pleasure of people by angering God, then God will leave him entrusted to the people."

36 Abū Ṭālib al-Makkī, *Qūt al-qulūb*, 2:233.

37 The verse is attributed to Salm al-Khāsir, *Dīwān*, 104.

Sahl [al-Tustarī] looked at one of his companions and ordered him to do something, he said,

> "Do this and that."
>
> The companion said, "O teacher, I am not capable of doing it because of the people."
>
> He turned to his companions and said, "No servant will achieve the truth of this matter [of improving himself] until he becomes one of two types: A servant who lets the people fall from his sight [i.e., forgets about people], and does not see anything in the world except his Creator, [and sees] that
> 316 no one is able to harm him | or benefit him. Then there is a servant whose own soul has fallen from his heart [i.e., he forgets the value of his soul], so he has no concern for the states they see him in."[38]

Al-Shāfiʿī رَحِمَهُ ٱللَّٰهُ said, "There is no one except that he has someone who loves him and someone who hates him. Since it is like this, be with the people who are obedient to God."[39]

It was said to Ḥasan [al-Baṣrī],

> "O Abū Saʿīd, people attend your gathering, and their intention is only to follow other than what you say and to annoy you with questions."
>
> He smiled and said to the speaker, "Be easy on yourself. I tell my soul about the residence in the garden and being close to the Merciful, then [my soul] desires it. I do not tell my soul [to find] safety with people because I know that their Creator and Provider, the One who gives them life and death, is not even safe from them [from their slights and insults]."[40]

Moses عَلَيْهِ ٱلسَّلَامُ said, "O my Lord, restrain the tongues of the people against me." [God] said, "O Moses, I have not chosen that for Myself, so why would I do it for you?"[41]

---

38 Abū Ṭālib al-Makkī, *Qūt al-qulūb*, 2:234.

39 Abū Nuʿaym, *Ḥilya*, 9:117.

40 Abū Ṭālib al-Makkī, *Qūt al-qulūb*, 2:234. The completion of his statement is, "So how can my soul find peace from them?"

41 Abū Ṭālib al-Makkī, *Qūt al-qulūb*, 2:234.

God سُبْحَانَهُ وَتَعَالَى revealed to Ezra (ʿUzayr), "If you are not personally delighted that I made you a morsel in the mouths of the people chewing, then I will not record you in my [record] as being among the humble."[42]

So, if someone confines himself in [his] house in order to improve people's opinions of him and statements about him, then he is in hardship dwelling only in this world. And the punishment of the hereafter is greater, if only they knew.[43] |

So retreat is not recommended except for one who devotes time 317
to his Lord in remembrance and reflection, in worship and [with gaining] knowledge. This is because if he were to mix with people, he would be wasting his time, increasing harm [to himself], and disturbing his acts of worship.

These are the hidden dangers in choosing retreat. It is appropriate to guard against them, for they are a means of destruction in the guise of deliverance.

The seventh benefit: [Gaining] experience

[Gaining experience] means benefiting from socializing with people and [following] the course of their states [i.e., going along with what people do]. The natural intellect (*ʿaql*) is insufficient to understand all the positive elements of the *dīn* and this world. Experience and practice bring benefit, and there is no good in retreat for someone who has not experienced trials.[44] Thus a young person who withdraws remains unsound [in judgment] and ignorant; it is appropriate that he engages in learning to attain, through a period of study, the experience he needs that would be sufficient for him. He can attain other experiences by hearing about them; thus he does not need to socialize.

Among the most important experiences is that he tests himself, his manners, and his inner qualities. This is not possible in seclusion. Each experience in seclusion is easy. When he is in seclusion, the evil consequence of each [incidence of] anger, malice, or envy is not brought up. These attributes are, in themselves, the means of destruction, and it is obligatory to overcome them and conquer

42 Abū Ṭālib al-Makkī, *Qūt al-qulūb*, 2:234.

43 This alludes to Qurʾān 39:26.

44 Ed note: That is, retreat is only useful for those who have experienced trials.

them. It is not sufficient to pacify them by distancing oneself from what instigates them. |

318 The example of the heart filled with these vile qualities is the example of an abscess filled with pus and decomposed matter. Perhaps one who has this [abscess] does not perceive the pain as long as it is not moved or touched. If he does not have a hand to touch it or an eye to see its form, and there is no one with him to move it, then he might think to himself that he is safe. He does not perceive the abscess in himself and is convinced it is not there. But, if something were to move it, or if the cupper were to puncture it with a lancet, then the pus would come out of it, and the fluid that had been prevented from flowing would flow out. Likewise, the heart filled with greed, malice, anger, jealousy, and other blameworthy qualities pours forth its vileness when agitated.

On this, the seekers on the path to the hereafter and those seeking the purification of [their] hearts must test themselves. If someone perceives arrogance in himself, he must strive to remove it, even to the point that he would carry a water sack on his back among people. Or he should carry wood on his head and bring it back to the markets [to sell]. He does this in order to test his soul. The wicked qualities of the soul and the plots of Satan are hidden, and only a few people are aware of them.

[About] this, it is reported that one [of the seekers] said,

> I repeated the prayers of thirty years, even though I had prayed them in the first row, because one day I was delayed with a [valid] excuse and I did not find a spot in the first row, so I stood in the second row. Then I found myself feeling shame from the looks people gave me, because [others] had preceded
> 319 me to the first row. Then I knew that all of my prayers | were tainted with ostentation and mixed with the delight [I felt] at people observing me and seeing me as among the foremost in doing good.

Socializing has a tremendous clear benefit in expelling vile qualities and overcoming them. [About] this it is said, "Travel exposes [one's] characteristics." This is because it is a type of continuous socializing.

The wicked qualities of thoughts and their subtle aspects will be discussed in the in the Rubᶜ al-Muhlikāt [Quarter of Perils].[45] Ignorance [regarding the effects of wicked thoughts] negates many good actions, while knowledge of [the effects] increases a small good deed. Were it not for that, there would be no virtue of knowledge over action; in that case, it would not be possible for the knowledge regarding prayer, when intended only for prayer, to be more virtuous than prayer [itself]. Certainly, we know that if something is intended for [something] other than itself, then that other thing is more noble than the thing itself. The law has determined the preference of the scholar (*ᶜālim*) over the worshiper (*ᶜābid*). On this point, [the Prophet] صَلَّى ٱللَّهُ عَلَيۡهِ وَسَلَّمَ said, "The virtue of the scholar over the worshiper is like my virtue over the lowest man among my Companions."[46]

The meaning of the virtue of knowledge is related to three aspects.

The first of them is what we have mentioned.

The second is the comprehensiveness of its benefit; the benefit [of knowledge] transcends [the scholar], whereas an action does not transcend [the worshiper].

The third is that the intended [meaning of the virtue of knowledge] is the knowledge of God, His attributes, and His actions, and that is more virtuous than any action. Moreover, the goal of actions is to distract hearts from the creation toward the Creator, so that after the distraction an awareness of Him and love for Him arises. So action and knowledge of the action is what is intended by this knowledge.

This knowledge is the ultimate goal of the novices (*murīd*), and [any] action is a condition for it. There is an indication of this in His
statement تَعَالَىٰ, | . . . *to Him ascends good speech, and righteous work* 320
raises it . . . [Q. 35:10]. Good speech is this knowledge, and righteous action is like one carrying and raising it toward its intended goal. So what is raised is more virtuous than what raises it.

This opposing argument [above] does not apply to these words [of God]. We refer to this intention with [the following] statement.

---

45 Ed. note: The Quarter of Perils consists of books 21–30 of al-Ghazālī's *Revival of the Religous Sciences* (*Iḥyāʾ ᶜulūm al-dīn*).

46 Al-Tirmidhī, *Sunan*, 2685.

If you know the benefits and dangers of retreat, then you realize that, in terms of preferring its negation or affirmation, it is a mistake to say that a ruling on [retreat] is universal. Rather, it is appropriate to look at the individual and his state, at those he associates with and their states, at the motive for his socializing and what is lost because of his socializing, [all in terms of] these above-mentioned benefits. Then what is lost can be compared to what is attained. At this [point] the truth will be elucidated and the preference made clear.

The words of al-Shāfiʿī رَضِيَ اللَّهُ عَنْهُ are the decisive statement [on the topic]. He said, "O Yūnus [b. ʿAbd al-Aʿlā l-Ṣadafī], withdrawing from people earns enmity, and joyfully embracing people attracts evil associates so be between withdrawing and embracing."[47]

It is obligatory to balance socializing and retreat and distinguish which [is best] based on conditions and by considering the benefits and harms that clarify the preference. This is the plain truth, and anything else said about it is deficient. Information for each person relates to the specific situation he is in, for it is not allowable to rule on one case [based on that of] someone else who is in a different state. |

321 The difference between the scholar and the Sufi in the manifestation of knowledge refers to this [point], that the Sufi talks only about his own state. So there is no avoiding differences in their responses to questions. The scholar is the one who comprehends the truth based on what he knows without looking at his own state. Thus he discloses the truth concerning [a question], and this is why there are no differences about [the response]. Thus the truth is always one, and there are many, [almost] unlimited, [who are] unable [to discern] the truth.

[In relation to] this, if a Sufi is asked about poverty (*faqr*), each one would answer with a response different from the response of another. All of that is true in relation to his state. It is not a [total] truth in itself since the truth is only one [in an absolute sense].

[In relation to] this, when Abū ʿAbdallāh al-Jalāʾ was asked about poverty, he said, "Strike your armor against a wall and say, 'My Lord is God.' That is poverty."[48]

---

47 Abū Nuʿaym, *Ḥilya*, 9:122.

48 Reported by al-Sarrāj (d. 378/988 or 989), *al-Lamaʿ*, 74. This indicates the perfection of withdrawal from the world and the verification of turning to God تَعَالَىٰ and taking refuge with Him. Al-Zabīdī, *Itḥāf*, 6:375.

Junayd said, "The destitute [person] (*faqīr*) is the one who does not ask anyone and does not confront anyone. If he is confronted, he stays silent."[49]

Sahl b. ʿAbdallāh [al-Tustarī] said, "The destitute [person] is the one who does not ask [from others] and does not accumulate [goods] ."[50]

Another one said, "It [destitution] is that there is nothing for you. And when it is for you, then it is not for you. | And hence, there is 322
nothing for you, there is nothing for you."[51]

Ibrāhīm al-Khawāṣṣ said, "[Destitution] is to abandon complaining and showing signs of being tested."[52]

The point is, if one hundred of [the Sufis] were asked, one hundred different answers would be heard. There is little chance that even two would agree. All of this is true in one aspect because it is information about the state of each person and what overwhelmed his heart. [In relation to] this, you do not see two of them such that one confirms that his companion is advancing in Sufism or praises him. Rather, each of them claims that he is persevering toward the truth and is familiar with it because most of their irresolution is based on the urgency of the states that confront their hearts. They are preoccupied only with their souls and do not pay any regard to others.

When the light of knowledge illuminates [something], it encompasses everything, unveils the curtain, and removes differences.

The example of the perception of these [Sufis] is similar to what you see in the perception of people on the proof of the sun's meridian by looking at the shadow. One of them says that in the summer [the shadow] is the length of two feet. Another reports that it is half a foot. Yet another refutes him and says that in the winter it is seven feet, while another report claims it is five feet. And there is still another to refute him. This is similar to the responses of the

49 Al-Sarrāj, *al-Lamaʿ*, 75.

50 Al-Sarrāj, *al-Lamaʿ*, 75. The narration states, "He does not ask, he does not refuse, and he does not obstruct."

51 Al-Sarrāj, *al-Lamaʿ*, 75. It is attributed to Ibn al-Jalāʾ who explains that destitution is the state of being poor and having no possessions, and immediately giving up any wealth or possessions he gains.

52 Al-Sarrāj, *al-Lamaʿ*, 75.

Sufis and their differences. Each one of them gives information about the shadow that he sees in his own land. So he is correct in his statement while another declares him in error because he thinks
323 that all of the world is like his land or similar to it. | So it is with a Sufi who judges the world based on his own state.

The astronomer [lit. scholar] knows [the time of] the meridian based on how long or short the shadow is and [knows] the reason for this difference in [other] lands. So he reports the different rulings for various lands. In some [lands], he says that [the meridian occurs] when no shadow remains, and in another [land] when [the shadow] lengthens. In yet another [land] it [occurs] when [the shadow] shortens. This is what we intended when we mentioned the preference for retreat or socializing.

So, if you said that whoever chooses retreat and sees it as preferable and safer for him then you must ask [about] the etiquette regarding retreat; we say that one must first take a long look at the etiquette of socializing, and we have already mentioned that in the book, *Kitāb ādāb al-ṣuḥba*.[53]

As for the etiquette of retreat, do not give it much consideration. It is appropriate for one [who has] withdrawn to first intend with his retreat to restrain his evil from people. Then, second, he [should] seek safety from all other evils.[54] Third, he [should seek] freedom from the harms of failing to fulfill the rights of Muslims. And fourth, [he should intend to] focus with the utmost concern on worshiping God. This is the etiquette of his intention.

Next, in his seclusion he [must be] diligent in [gaining] knowledge and [undertaking] action, and [in] remembrance and reflection, in
324 order to reap | the fruits of retreat. He must prevent people from increasing their intrusions [on] and visits to him, for then his time will be wasted. He must hold back from questioning [them] about

53 Book 15 of the *Revival of the Religious Sciences: The Proprieties of Friendship and Brotherhood.*

54 Al-Ghazālī used the expression "from all other evils" (*min sharr al-ashrār*) and not the expression "from their evil" (*min sharrihim*). This indicates that not every associate is evil. Thus, one does not seek safety from him because there is no evil from him. This is a good cautious approach. It may be understood that "from their evil" means "from the evil of their evils" (*min sharr ashrārihim*). Al-Zabīdī, *Itḥāf*, 6:377.

their news and listening to rumors spreading in the land, and what people are preoccupied with. All of that sinks into the heart until it emerges during prayer or reflection when least expected. The status of news that reaches the ear is like the status of a seed in the ground. It must grow, and its roots and branches spread out. Thus [one rumor] evokes another. An important concern for one in retreat is cutting off the whisperings (*wasāwis*) that distract from the remembrance of God. Such news is the spring and source of whisperings.

He [must also be] content with a simple life, otherwise he would be compelled to have recourse to people and be in need of socializing [with] them.

[One in retreat must also] be patient with the harm that comes to him from neighbors. He must stop himself from listening to praise about him [going into] retreat or reproach of him for abandoning socializing. All of that effects the heart, even if only for a short time. The state of the hearts' preoccupation will necessarily be an obstacle on his journey on the path of the hereafter. The journey is either through diligence in the litany (*wird*) and remembrance with presence of heart, or it is through reflection on the majesty of God, His attributes, His actions and dominion over His heavens and His earth, or it is through contemplation on the subtleties of actions, [what] corrupts hearts, and seeking ways to protect from [what corrupts]. All of this requires to a clear mind [lit., void (*farāgh*)] and attentiveness to anything that confuses the heart in that state. The memory of it [what preoccupies the heart] is revived, and if continually recalled [will come to mind] when not expected.

He [must also] have a righteous wife or righteous companion so that his soul finds rest with her/him for some time during the
day | from the fatigue of diligence. This is an aid for the remainder 325
of the time [in retreat].

Patience is incomplete in retreat unless he severs the desire for this world and what people are engaged in. There can be no severing of his desire except by diminishing [his] expectation, as he should not presume that he will have a long life. Rather, when morning comes to him, [he should know] he may have no evening, and when evening comes to him, he may have no morning. Thus it is easy for him to have patience for a day, but it is not easy for him to maintain [this] patience for twenty years, or [even] if taking into account a lesser time.

[The one in retreat] must also give much thought to death and the loneliness of the grave whenever his heart is contrained by solitude. He [must] realize that whoever has not attained in his heart the remembrance of God and gnosis (*maʿrifa*) of Him will not be familiar with Him and cannot endure the desolation of solitude after death. Whoever is familiar with the remembrance of God and gnosis of Him, death will not remove that familiarity. For death does not destroy the state of familiarity and gnosis; indeed he will remain alive in the gnosis and familiarity of Him. [Indeed] he will be joyous with the grace and mercy of God on him, just as God تَعَالَىٰ says about the martyrs, *And never think of those who have been killed in the cause of God as dead. Rather, they are alive with their Lord, receiving provision, rejoicing in what God has bestowed on them of His bounty...* [Q. 3:169–170]. Each person fully devoted to God in the struggle with himself is a martyr when death overtakes him, [because of his] acceptance and [because he] did not flee [from] it. The one who strives (*mujāhid*) strives against himself and his desires. The Messenger of God صَلَّى ٱللَّهُ عَلَيْهِ وَسَلَّمَ made this clear. The greater struggle
326 is the struggle against the soul.[55] | Like the Companions رَضِيَ ٱللَّهُ عَنْهُمْ said, "We have returned from the lesser struggle to the greater struggle."[56] They mean the struggle against the soul.

55 Al-Tirmidhī, *Sunan*, 1621; Ibn Ḥibbān, *Ṣaḥīḥ*, 4624; Ibn Ḥanbal, *Musnad*, 6:20; al-Ḥākim al-Nīsābūrī, *al-Mustadrak*, 1:11; al-Ṭabarānī, *al-Muʿjam al-kabīr*, 18:309.

56 Al-Bayhaqī, *al-Zuhd al-kabīr*, 373; al-Khaṭīb al-Baghdādī, *Tārīkh Baghdād*, 13:498; Ibn al-Jawzī, *Dhamm al-hawā*, 118, from Jābir b. ʿAbdallāh رَضِيَ ٱللَّهُ عَنْهُ as attributed to the Prophet صَلَّى ٱللَّهُ عَلَيْهِ وَسَلَّمَ. The wording of the narration is, "You have come in the best way. You have come from the lesser struggle to the greater struggle." They asked, "What is the greater struggle?" He said, "The struggle of the servant against his desire."

This completes the Book of the *Proprieties of Retreat*, book 16 of the Quarter of Customs from the *Revival of the Religious Sciences*. All praise is due to God, the Lord of the worlds. Blessings and peace be on His Messenger Muḥammad, and on his good and pure family, and on all of his Companions. The Book of the *Proprieties of Travel* (*Kitāb ādāb al-safar*) follows [book 17 of the Quarter of Customs from the *Revival of the Religious Sciences*].

Bibliography

Works in Western Languages

al-Ghazālī, Abū Ḥāmid Muḥammad b. Muḥammad. *The Book of Knowledge: Kitāb al-ʿilm. Book 1 of The Revival of the Religious Sciences*. Translated by Kenneth Honerkamp. Louisville, KY: Fons Vitae, 2015.

Schimmel, Annemarie. *Mystical Dimensions of Islam*, Chapel Hill: University of North Carolina Press, 1975.

Walzer, R. "Djālīnūs." In *Encyclopaedia of Islam*, second edition. Leiden: E. J. Brill, 1965, 2:402–403.

Works in Arabic

ʿAbd al-Razzāq b. Hammām al-Ṣanʿānī. *al-Muṣannaf*. Edited by Ḥabīb al-Raḥmān al-ʿAẓamī. Beirut: al-Maktab al-Islāmī, 1983.

Abū Dāwūd, Sulaymān b. al-Ashaʿth al-Sijistānī. *Sunan Abī Dāwūd*. Edited by ʿIzzat ʿAbīd al-Daʿās and ʿĀdil al-Sayyid. Beirut: Dār Ibn Ḥazm, 1997.

Abū Nuʿaym al-Iṣbahānī, Aḥmad b. ʿAbdallāh. *Ḥilya al-awliyāʾ wa-ṭabaqāt al-aṣfiyāʾ*. Cairo: Maṭbaʿāt al-Saʿāda wa-l-Khānijī, 1357/1938; repr. Beirut: Dār al-Kitāb al-ʿArabī, 1987.

———. *Maʿrifat al-ṣaḥāba*. Riyadh: Dār al-Waṭan, 1998.

Abū Ṭālib al-Makkī, Muḥammad b. ʿAlī. *Qūt al-qulūb*. Edited by Muḥammad al-Zaharī l-Ghumurāwī. Cairo: al-Maṭbaʿat al-Maymaniyya, 1310/1893; repr. Beirut: Dār Ṣādir/Dār al-Fikr, n.d.

Abū Yaʿlā, Aḥmad b. ʿAlī. *Musnad Abī Yaʿlā l-Mawṣūlī*. Edited by Ḥusayn Salīm Asad al-Dārānī. Damascus: Dār al-Maʾmūn li-l-Turāth and Dār al-Thaqāfa al-ʿArabiyya, 1989.

Aḥmad b. Ḥanbal. *See under* Ibn Ḥanbal.

al-Ājurī, Muḥammad b. al-Ḥusayn. *al-Sharīʿa*. Beirut: Muʾassasat al-Rayyān, 2008.

ʿAlī b. Abī Ṭālib. *Anwār al-ʿuqūl li-waṣī l-rasūl* (also known as *Dīwān al-imām ʿAlī b. Abī Ṭālib*). Edited by ʿAbd al-Majīd Hamū. Beirut: Dār Ṣādir, 2010.

ʿAlī b. al-Jahm. *Dīwān Ibn al-Jahm*. Edited by Khalīl Mardam. Beirut: Dār Ṣādir, 1996.

al-Azraqī, Muḥammad b. ʿAbdallāh. *Akhbār Makka wa-mā fīhā min al-āthār*. Edited by ʿAlī ʿUmar. Cairo: Maktabat al-Thaqāfat al-Dīniyya, 2004.

al-Bayhaqī, Aḥmad b. al-Ḥusayn. *Dalāʾil al-nubuwwa wa-maʿrifa aḥwāl ṣāḥib al-sharīʿa*. Edited by ʿAbd al-Muʿṭī Qalʿajī. Cairo: Dār al-Rayyān and Beirut: Dār al-Kutub al-ʿIlmiyya, 1988.

——. *al-Jāmiʿ li-shuʿab al-īmān*. Edited by ʿAbd al-ʿAlī ʿAbd al-Ḥamīd Ḥāmid and Mukhtār Aḥmad al-Nadawī. Riyad: Maktabat al-Rushd, 1423/2003.

——. *al-Sunan al-kubrā*. Beirut: Dār al-Maʿrifa, 1356.

——. *al-Zuhd al-kabīr*. Edited by ʿĀmir Aḥmad Ḥaydar. Beirut: Muʾassasat al-Kutub al-Thaqāfiyya, 1996.

al-Bukhārī, Muḥammad b. Ismāʿīl. *Ṣaḥīḥ al-Bukhārī*. 9 vols. Cairo: Būlāq, 1311–13; repr. Beirut: Dār Ṭawq al-Najāt, 1422/2001.

al-Daylamī, Shīrawayh b. Shahdār. *al-Firdaws bi-maʾthūr al-khiṭṭāb = Musnad al-firdaws*. Edited by Saʿīd b. Basyūnī Zaghlūl. 6 vols. Beirut: Dār al-Kutub al-ʿIlmiyya, 1986.

al-Dīnawarī, Aḥmad b. Marwān b. Muḥammad. *al-Majālisa wa-jawāhir al-ʿilm*. Beirut: Dār Ibn Ḥazm, 2002.

al-Faryābī, Jaʿfar b. Muḥammad. *Ṣifat al-nifāq wa-dhamm al-munāfiqīn*. Edited by ʿAbd al-Raqīb b. ʿAlī. Beirut: Dār Ibn Zaydūn, 1990.

al-Ghazālī, Abū Ḥāmid Muḥammad b. Muḥammad. *Iḥyāʾ ʿulūm al-dīn*. 9 vols., vol. 10 not numbered.] Jedda: Dār al-Minhāj, 2011.

——. *Mīzān al-ʿamal*. Edited by Sulaymān Dunyā. Cairo: Dār al-Maʿārif, 1964.

al-Ḥākim al-Nīsābūrī, Muḥammad b. ʿAbdallāh. *al-Mustadrak ʿalā l-Ṣaḥīḥayn*. 5 vols. Hyderabad: Daʾirat al-Maʿārif al-Niẓāmiyya, 1335/1917; repr. Beirut: Dār al-Maʿrifa, n.d.

Hannād b. al-Sirrī b. Mūsā l-Dārimī l-Kūfī. *al-Zuhd*. Edited by ʿAbd al-Raḥmān b. ʿAbd al-Jabbār al-Firiyawāʾī. Kuwait: Dār al-Khulafāʾ li-l-Kitāb al-Islāmī, 1406/1986.

Ibn ʿAbd al-Barr, Yūsuf b. ʿAbdallāh. *Jāmiʿ bayān al-ʿilm wa-faḍlih*. Edited by Abū l-Ashbāl al-Zuhayrī. Riyadh: Dār Ibn al-Jawzī, 1994.

——. *al-Tamhīd*. Casablanca: Wizārat al-Awqāf, 1967.

Ibn Abī l-Dunyā, ʿAbdallāh b. Muḥammad al-Qurashī. *Mudārāt al-nās*. Edited by Muḥammad Khayr Ramaḍān Yūsuf. Beirut: Dār Ibn Ḥazm, 1998.

——. *al-ʿUzla wa-l-infirād*. Edited by Mashūr b. Ḥasan Āl Salmān. Riyadh: Dār al-Waṭan, 1997.

Ibn Abī l-Ḥadīd = ʿAbd al-Ḥamīd b. Hibatallāh b. Muḥammad. *Sharḥ nahj al-balāgha*. Edited by Muḥammad Abū l-Faḍl Ibrāhīm. Cairo: Dār Iḥyāʾ al-Kutub al-ʿArabiyya, n.d.

Ibn Abī Shayba, ʿAbdallāh b. Muḥammad. *al-Muṣannaf*. Edited by Muḥammad ʿAwāmma. 26 vols. Jedda: Dār al-Minhāj, 2006.

Ibn ʿAdī = ʿAbdallāh b. ʿAdī l-Jurjānī. *al-Kāmil fī ḍuʿafāʾ al-rijāl*. First printing edited by Suhayl Zakkār and third printing edited by Yaḥyā Mukhtār Ghazāwī. Beirut: Dār al-Fikr, 1988.

Ibn ʿAsākir, ʿAlī b. al-Ḥasan. *Tārīkh madīnat Dimashq*. Edited by Muḥibb al-Dīn ʿUmar b. Gharāma al-ʿUmrāwī. 80 vols. Beirut: Dār al-Fikr, 1995.

Ibn Ḥanbal = Aḥmad b. Ḥanbal. *Musnad al-Imām Aḥmad b. Ḥanbal*. Edited by Shuʿayb al-Arnāʾūṭ. Beirut: Muʾassasat al-Risāla, 1995.

Ibn Ḥibbān = Muḥammad b. Ḥibbān al-Bustī. *Rawḍat al-ʿuqalāʾ*. Edited by ʿAbd al-ʿAlīm Muḥammad al-Darwīsh. Damascus: al-Hayʾa al-ʿĀmma al-Sūriyya lil-Kitāb, 2009.

——. *Ṣaḥīḥ ibn Ḥibbān = al-Musnad al-ṣaḥīḥ ʿalā l-taqāsīm wa-l-ānwāʿ*. [Rearranged by ʿAlī b. Balbān al-Fārisī l-Maṣrī under the title *al-Iḥsān fī taqrīb ṣaḥīḥ Ibn Ḥibbān*] Edited by Shuʿayb al-Arnaʾūṭ. 18 vols. Beirut: Muʿassasa al-Risāla, 1997.

Ibn al-Jawzī, ʿAbd al-Raḥmān b. ʿAlī. *Dhamm al-hawā*. Edited by Khālid ʿAbd al-Laṭīf. Beirut: Dār al-Kitāb al-ʿArabī, 2009.

——.*Ṣifat al-ṣafwa*. Edited by ʿAbd al-Salām Hārūn. Beirut: Muʾassassa al-Kutub al-Thaqāfiyya, 1992.

Ibn Mājah, Muḥammad b. Yazīd. *Sunan Ibn Mājah*. Edited by Muḥammad Fuʾād ʿAbd al-Bāqī. Cairo: Dār Iḥyāʾ al-Kutub al-ʿArabiyya, 1954.

Ibn al-Mubārak, ʿAbdallāh. *al-Zuhd wa-l-raqāʾiq bi-riwayat al-Marūzī*. Edited by Ḥabīb al-Raḥmān al-ʿAẓamī; repr. Beirut: Dār al-Kutub al-ʿIlmiyya, n.d.

Ibn Qutayba al-Dīnawarī, ʿAbdallāh b. Muslim. *ʿUyūn al-akhbār*. 4 vols. Cairo: Dār al-Kutub al-Miṣriyya, 1930.

Ibn al-Rūmī, ʿAlī b. al-ʿAbbās b. Jurayj. *Dīwān Ibn al-Rūmī*. Edited by Ḥusayn Niṣār. Cairo: Dār al-Kutub wa-l-Wathāʾiq al-Qawmiyya, 2003.

Ibn Saʿd = Muḥammad b. Saʿd al-Baṣrī. *Ṭabaqāt al-kabīr*. Edited by ʿAlī Muḥammad ʿUmar. 11 vols. Cairo: Maktabat al-Khanjī, 2001.

Ibn al-Ṣalāḥ, ʿUthmān b. ʿAbd al-Raḥmān. *Muqaddima Ibn al-Ṣalāḥ wa-maḥāsin al-iṣṭilāḥ*. Edited by ʿĀʾisha ʿAbd al-Raḥmān. Cairo: Dār al-Maʿārif, 1989.

al-ʿIrāqī, Zayn al-Dīn Abū l-Faḍl ʿAbd al-Raḥīm b. al-Ḥusayn. *al-Mughnī ʿan ḥaml al-asfār fī takhrīj mā fī l-iḥyāʾ min al-akhbār*. Riyadh: Maktaba Dār Ṭābiriyya, 1415/1995.

al-Kalābādhī, Muḥammad b. Ibrāhīm. *al-Taʿarruf li-madhhab ahl al-taṣawwuf*. Edited by ʿAbd al-Ḥalīm Muḥammad and Ṭaha ʿAbd al-Bāqī Surūr. Damascus: Dār al-Īmān, 1986.

al-Khaṭīb al-Baghdādī, Aḥmad b. ʿAlī. *Sharaf aṣḥāb al-ḥadīth*. Edited by Muḥammad Saʿīd Khaṭīb Ughlī. Ankara: Jāmiʿat Anqara, Kulliyya al-Ilāhiyyāt, n.d.

——.*Tārīkh Baghdād*. Edited by Muṣṭafā ʿAbd al-Qādir ʿAṭā. 24 vols. Beirut: Dār al-Kutub al-ʿIlmiyya, 1997.

al-Khaṭṭābī, Abū Sulaymān Ḥamd b. Muḥammad. *al-ʿUzla*. Edited by Muḥammad Munīr al-Dimashqī. Cairo: Idārāt al-Ṭibāʿa al-Munīriyya, 1352.

Majnūn Laylā = Qays b. al-Mulawwaḥ. *Dīwān majnūn laylā*. Edited by ʿAbd al-Sattār Aḥmad Farāj. Cairo: Dār Miṣr li-l-Ṭibāʿa, n.d.

al-Makkī, Abū Ṭālib. *See under* Abū Ṭālib al-Makkī.

Mālik b. Anas. *al-Muwaṭṭaʾ*. Edited by Muḥammad Fuʾād ʿAbd al-Bāqī. Cairo: Dār Iḥyāʾ al-Kutub al-ʿArabiyya, n.d.

al-Mubarrad, Muḥammad b. Yazīd. *al-Kāmil*. Edited by Muḥammad Aḥmad al-Dālī. Beirut: Muʾassasat al-Risāla, 1997.

al-Munāwī, Muḥammad ʿAbd al-Raʾūf b. ʿAlī. *Fayḍ al-qadīr sharḥ al-jāmiʿ al-ṣaghīr*. Beirut: Dār al-Maʿrifa, 1357/[1938].

Muslim b. al-Ḥajjāj al-Qushayrī l-Nīsābūrī. *al-Jāmiʿ al-ṣaḥīḥ = Ṣaḥīḥ Muslim*. Edited by Muḥammad Fuʾād ʿAbd al-Bāqī. 5 vols. Cairo and Beirut: Dār Iḥyāʾ al-Kutub al-ʿArabiyya, 1954.

al-Nasāʾī, Aḥmad b. Shuʿayb. *Kitāb al-sunan al-kubrā*. Edited by Shuʿayb al-Arnaʾūṭ and Ḥasan ʿAbd al-Munʿim Shālbī. 12 vols. Beirut: Muʿassasa al-Risāla, 2001.

———. *Sunan al-Nasāʾī (al-mujtabā)*. Cairo: al-Maṭbaʿat al-Maymūniyya, 1312/1894; repr. Beirut: Dār al-Kitāb al-ʿArabī.

Qays b. Dharīḥ al-Kinānī. *Dīwān qays lubnā*. Edited by Ḥusayn Niṣār. Cairo: Dār Miṣr li-l-Ṭabāʿa, n.d.

al-Qushayrī, ʿAbd al-Karīm. *al-Risāla al-Qushayriyya*. Edited by ʿAbd al-Ḥalīm Maḥmūd and Maḥmūd b. al-Sharīf. Cairo: Dār al-Shaʿab, 1989.

Salm b. ʿAmr al-Khāsir. *Dīwān Salm al-Khāsir (ḍammana Shuʿarāʾ ʿabbāsiyyūn li-gharūnbāwm)*. Edited by Muḥammad Yūsuf Najm and Dr. Iḥsān ʿAbbās. Beirut: Dār Maktabat al-Ḥayyā, 1959.

al-Sarrāj, Abū Naṣr ʿAbdallāh b. ʿAlī l-Ṭūsī. *al-Lamaʿ*. Edited by ʿAbd al-Ḥalīm Maḥmūd and Ṭaha ʿAbd al-Bāqī Surūr. Cairo and Baghdad: Dār al-Kutub al-Ḥadītha wa-Maktabat al-Muthannā, 1380/1960.

al-Ṭabarānī, Sulaymān b. Aḥmad. *al-Muʿjam al-awsāṭ*. 10 vols. Cairo: Dār al-Ḥaramayn, 1995.

———. *al-Muʿjam al-kabīr*. Edited by Ḥamdī ʿAbd al-Majīd al-Salafī. Beirut: Dār Iḥyāʾ al-Turāth al-ʿArabī, n.d.

al-Ṭayālisī, Abū Dāwūd Sulaymān b. Dāwud. *Musnad Abī Dāwud al-Ṭayālisī*. Beirut: Dār al-Maʿrifa, 1321/1903.

al-Tirmidhī, Muḥammad b. ʿĪsā. *Sunan al-Tirmidhī = al-Jāmiʿ al-ṣaḥīḥ*. Edited by Aḥmad Shākir, Muḥammad Fuʾād ʿAbd al-Bāqī, and Ibrāhīm ʿAṭwa. 5 vols. Beirut: Dār Iḥyāʾ al-Turāth al-ʿArabī, n.d.; repr of Cairo, 1938 edition.

al-ʿUkbarī, ʿAbdallāh b. al-Ḥusayn. *al-Tibyān fī sharḥ al-dīwān = Sharḥ Dīwān al-Mutanabbī*. Edited by Muṣṭafā l-Saqā, Ibrāhīm al-Ībārī, and ʿAbd al-Ḥafīẓ Shalabī. Cairo: Maktabat wa-Maṭbaʿāt Muṣṭafā l-Bābī l-Ḥalabī, 1971.

ʿUmāra b. ʿAqīl. *Dīwān ʿumāra b. ʿaqīl*. Edited by Shākir al-ʿĀshūr. Basra: Maṭbaʿa al-Baṣra, 1973.

al-Washāʾ, Muḥammad b. Aḥmad. *al-Mawshā aw al-ẓarf wa-l-ẓurafāʾ*. Edited by Kamāl Muṣṭafā. Cairo: Maktabat al-Khānjī, 1993.

al-Yāfiʿī (d. 768/1366 or 1367), ʿAbdallāh b. Asʿad b. ʿAlī. *al-Irshād wa-l-taṭrīz fī faḍl dhikr Allāh wa-tilāwat kitābihi al-ʿazīz wa-faḍl al-awliyāʾ wa-l-nāsikīn wa-l-fuqarāʾ wa-l-masākīn*. Edited by Anas Muḥammad ʿAdnān al-Sharafāwī. Jedda: Dār al-Minhāj, 2007.

al-Zabīdī, Muḥammad Murtaḍā, *Itḥāf al-sādat al-muttaqīn bi-sharḥ Iḥyāʾ ʿulūm al-dīn*. 10 vols. [Cairo]: al-Maṭbaʿat al-Maymūniyya, 1311/1894.

Index of Qurʾānic Verses

Index of *Ḥadīth*

The believer, the one who struggles against himself and [with] his wealth in the cause of God, 15
The believer is the one who is friendly and is taken as a friend…, 8
The believer who socializes with people and is patient with their offenses…, 16
Beware of backbiting, for backbiting is more severe than fornication or adultery, 36 n.55

The example of a person who sits and listens to wisdom but then acts only according to any evil he hears is like the example, 35
The example of the gathering of evil is the example of the [blacksmith's] bellow. The harm from it will either burn you or its smell will affect you, 34

From these used vessels, seek blessings from the hands of the Muslims, 13

Gabriel came to the Prophet and gave him a choice between this world and the hereafter. [The Prophet] chose the hereafter over this world, 40
God loves the servant who is pious, [financially] independent, and unknown, 15
God said, "When I test My servant concerning his eyes, and he is patient, I will give him paradise as a replacement for them," 48 n.97
The greater struggle is the struggle against the soul, 72

[He is] a man who [directs] the reins of his horse in the cause of God, anticipating that he will be victorious or be defeated, 16

If any one of you remains patient in some abode of Islam, then that is better for him than any one of you worshiping alone for forty years, 12
If someone breaks the staff of the Muslims while the Muslims are united in Islam, then he has removed the rope of Islam from his neck, 9

If someone seeks the pleasure of God by angering people, then God will suffice him against the burden of the people, 63 n.35
If someone separates from the congregation and dies, then his death is [like a death in the time of] ignorance (*jāhiliyya*), 9
Indeed, God does not become weary until you are weary, 59
I seek the blessing of the hands of the Muslims, 14 n.43
It is a time when a man is not safe from the one sitting next to him, 38–39
It is not allowed for a Muslim to abandon his brother for more than three [days]. The one who is first [to end the separation] enters paradise, 9
It is not permissible for a Muslim to abandon his brother for more than three days unless there is no safety against his misfortunes, 11
It was reported that when the [Messenger of God] circumambulated the House [i.e., the Kaʿba], he went toward the well of Zamzam to drink from it…, 13–14

Look to the one who is beneath you and do not look to the one who is above you. It is not suitable to scorn the bounty God [gave] you, 46

A man [follows] the *dīn* of his intimate friend, so each of you must consider the one with whom he forms an intimate friendship, 59

The owner of a thing has more duty to carry it, 63

Satan is a wolf among people, like a wolf among sheep. He comes from afar and from the side, and he comes for the stray one, 12
… The station of any one of you going out in the cause of God is better than his praying in his house for sixty years…, 12

That your house suffices you, you restrain your tongue [so as to not harm] yourself, and you cry over your mistakes, 15
There will soon be a time when the best wealth of a Muslim will be sheep that he takes to the tops of the mountains, 37
A time will come when there is no safety for one who has *dīn*, 38

The virtue of the scholar over the worshiper is like my virtue over the lowest man among my Companions, 67

Were I to take an intimate friend, then I would take Abū Bakr as an intimate friend. But your companion [i.e., the Prophet] is the intimate friend of God, 19
When the people see an evil act, but do not change it, then soon God will send punishment to them all, 26
Whoever abandons his brother for a year is like one who has shed his blood, 10

Index of People and Places

Subject Index

About the Translator

James Pavlin recieved his PhD from New York University. He is an adjunct professor in the history department at William Paterson University (New Jersey) and a part time lecturer in the department of religion at Rutgers University. He is the author of *Ibn Taymiya's Epistle on Worship: Risālat al-ʿubūdiyya*. He has written extensively on Muslim creed, theology, and *kalām*, and their relation to Islamic philosophy. He has also translated several other books of the *Revival of the Religious Sciences* (*Iḥyāʾ ʿulūm al-dīn*), these include *The Etiquette of the Recitation of the Qurʾān* (book 8), *The Proprieties of Friendship and Brotherhood* (book 15), and *The Commanding of Right and the Forbidding of Wrong* (book 19).